ON THE FRONT LINES:
A PRACTICAL GUIDE FOR INSTRUCTORS OF DEVELOPMENTAL ENGLISH

Donna Bontatibus
Middlesex Community College

Longman

Boston   Columbus   Indianapolis   New York   San Francisco   Upper Saddle River   Amsterdam
Cape Town   Dubai   London   Toronto   Madrid   Milan   Munich   Paris   Montreal   Toronto
Delhi   Mexico City   Sao Paulo   Sydney   Hong Kong   Seoul   Singapore   Taipei   Tokyo

On the Front Lines: A Practical Guide for Instructors of Developmental English

Copyright ©2011 Pearson Education, Inc.

1 2 3 4 5 6 7 8 9 10   12 11 10 09

Longman is an
imprint of

www.pearsonhighered.com

ISBN-10: 0-205-81680-0

ISBN-13 978-0-205-81680-4

TABLE OF CONTENTS

INTRODUCTION

On the Front Lines is a practical, streamlined guide designed for the instructors—new, adjunct, temporary, and even seasoned—of developmental writing at the community college. Within eight concise chapters, instructors receive realistic, easy-to-apply advice that centers on the preparation and teaching of developmental writing in a nation with over 1,000 community colleges. Instructors will be walked through the process of preparing a syllabus; structuring the classroom experience; appealing to different learning styles; teaching with technology; constructing and evaluating assignments; and conferencing with students. This accessible guide also encourages instructors to look outside the classroom—to familiarize themselves with campus resources and policies that support the classroom experience—and to look ahead for their own professional development opportunities. Given the debates on developmental education and the importance of first-year experience initiatives to assist with student transition and retention, there is a monumental amount of weight placed on the shoulders of instructors of developmental writing. *On the Front Lines* respects the instructor's role in the developmental writing classroom and offers practical, straightforward guidance to see the instructor through the preparation of classes to the submission of final grades.

ACKNOWLEDGEMENTS

I would like to thank the following professors served as reviewers for *On the Front Lines*:

Sonya L. Armstrong, Northern Illinois University
Shanti Bruce, Nova Southeastern University
Jonathan Bush, Western Michigan University
Kelly, Chesnutt, Everest College
David Elias, Eastern Kentucky University
Stella Fox, Nassau Community College
Lewis J. Kahler, Mohawk Valley Community College
Lisa B. Martin, Piedmont Technical College
Kathryn Swanson, Augsburg College

Donna Bontatibus
Middlesex Community College

Developmental Writing
Student & Instructor Supplements

Student Supplements

The Pearson Lab Manual for Developing Writers (Sentences 0-205-63409-5/ Paragraphs 0-205-69341-5/ Essays: 0-205-69340-7)
This three-volume workbook is an ideal supplement for any developmental writing sequence. References direct students to Pearson's MyWritingLab, the marketing-leading online practice system, for even more practice.
 • **Volume A: Sentences (0-205-63409-5)**
At this level, exercises and applications of grammar, punctuation and mechanics stress rules rather than simply skill and drill. There are many composing exercises that apply sentence skills explained in the students' primary textbook.
 • **Volume B: Paragraphs (0-205-69341-5) & Volume C: Essays (0-205-69340-7)**
The exercises encourage students to apply key concepts covered in most writing classes—i.e. topic sentences, thesis statements, coherence, unity, levels of development. *Analysis* exercises give further illustration of concepts explained in class and in the primary textbook; *Building* exercises give students the "raw materials" to develop paragraphs and/or essays along the various modes. Revision prompts encourage students to look at specific key elements of their own writing and assess whether they have met the needs of their reading audience.

The Pearson Student Essays Booklet (0-205-60544-3)
This brief booklet of student models includes two essays from each of the nine modes. It also includes an essay that showcases the writing process from beginning to end, crystallizing the importance of revision for all writers.

Pearson Visual Writing Guide for Developing Writers by Ileen L. Linden (0-205-61984-3)
The Pearson Visual Writing Guide for Developing Writers is a thematic supplement designed to stimulate reading comprehension through an authentic perspective of visual imagery. Each assignment challenges the learner to think beyond the text to the image, expanding their worldview as they navigate through complex or unfamiliar issues. This approach teaches deconstruction, a problem-based strategy that reveals important social and cultural interrelationships across the curriculum. Instructors will find this a practical guide for assignments directed toward journaling, reflection, argumentative essay writing and more.

100 Things to Write About by Ron Koertge (0-673-98239-4)
This brief book contains over 100 individual writing assignments, on a variety of topics and in a wide range of formats, from expressive to analytical writing.

The Pearson Student Planner (0-205-66301-X)
This unique supplement provides students with a space to plan, think about, and present their work. In addition to the yearly planner, this portfolio includes an assessing/organizing area, daily planner for students including daily, weekly, and monthly calendars, and a useful links page.

The Pearson Writer's Journal and Student Planner by Mimi Markus (0-205-64665-4)
This supplement gives students a place to explore their own writing in the writer's journal section while also giving them space to stay organized in the student planner section. The journal portion of the supplement guides students' writing through prewriting strategies, suggested themes for their journal writing, and sample student entries. In the planner section, students can use the monthly, weekly, and daily calendars to effectively manage their time and their course assignments.

Applying English to Your Career by Deborah Davis (0-131-92115-0)
This supplement includes a brief page of instruction on 25 key writing skills, followed by practice exercises in these skills that focus on seven specific career fields.

The New American Webster Handy College Dictionary, 3/e (0-451-18166-2)
A paperback reference text with more than 100,000 entries.

The Oxford American Desk Dictionary and Thesaurus (0-425-18068-9)
From the Oxford University Press and Berkley Publishing Group comes this one-of-a-kind reference book that combines both of the essential language tools—dictionary and thesaurus—in a single, integrated A-to-Z volume. The 1,024 page book offers more than 150,000 entries, definitions, and synonyms so you can find the right word every time, as well as appendices of valuable quick-reference information including: signs and symbols, weights and measures, presidents of the U.S., U.S. states and capitals, and more.

The Oxford Essential Thesaurus (0-425-16421-7)
From Oxford University Press, renowned for quality educational and reference works, comes this concise, easy-to-use thesaurus - the essential tool for finding just the right word for every occasion. The 528 page book includes 175,000 synonyms in a simple A-to-Z format, more than 10,000 entries, extensive word choices, example sentences and phrases, and guidance on usage, punctuation.

The Pearson ESL Workbook, 2/e by Susan Miller and Karen Standridge (0-131-94759-1)
This workbook is divided into seven major units, each of which provides thorough explanations and exercises in the most challenging grammar topics for non-native speakers of English. Topics include nouns, articles, verbs, modifiers, pronouns, prepositions, and sentence structure.

Eighty Practices by Maxine Hairston Emerita (0-673-53422-7)
A collection of ten-item exercises that provide additional practice for specific grammatical usage problems, such as comma splices, capitalization, and pronouns.

The Pearson Grammar Workbook, 2/e by Jeanette Adkins (0-131-94771-0)
This workbook is a comprehensive source of instruction for students who need additional grammar, punctuation, and mechanics assistance. Covering such topics as subject-verb agreement, conjunctions, modifiers, capital letters, and vocabulary, each chapter provides helpful explanations, examples, and exercises.

Learning Together: An Introduction to Collaborative Learning by Tori Haring-Smith (0-673-46848-8)
This brief guide to the fundamentals of collaborative learning teaches students how to work effectively in groups.

Pearson Editing Exercises, 2/e (Student / 0-205-66618-3, Instructor Answer Key / 0-205-66617-5)
The Editing Exercises booklet contains fifty one-page editing paragraphs that provide students with opportunities to learn how to recognize and correct the most common types of sentence, grammar, and mechanical errors in context. Embedding the errors within the context of informative paragraphs rather than using discrete sentence exercises simulates a more natural writing situation, allowing students to draw upon their intuitive knowledge of structure and syntax, as well as specific information from class instruction. The booklet makes an ideal supplement to any grammar, sentence, or writing text. Various editing topics can be assigned to coordinate with class lessons, or they may be assigned individually based on problems observed in students' writing. Students may also complete selected exercises as an enrichment activity, either on their own or in collaboration with other students. Additionally, the variety of topics in the paragraphs themselves can also be used as springboards for discussion or journaling, or as models for writing assignments if desired.

Penguin Discount Novel Program

In cooperation with Penguin Putnam, Inc., Pearson is proud to offer a variety of Penguin paperbacks at a significant discount when packaged with any Pearson title. Excellent additions to any English course, Penguin titles give students the opportunity to explore contemporary and classical fiction and drama. The available titles include works by authors as diverse as Toni Morrison, Julia Alvarez, Mary Shelley, and Shakespeare. To review the complete list of titles available, visit the Pearson-Penguin-Putnam website: http://www.pearsonhighered.com/penguin.

What Every Student Should Know About (WESSKA) Series

The **What Every Student Should Know About...** series is a collection of guide books designed to help students with specific topics that are important in a number of different college courses. Instructors can package any one of these booklets with their Pearson textbook for no additional charge, or the booklets can be purchased separately.

What Every Student Should Know About Preparing Effective Oral Presentations (0-205-50545-7)
Martin R. Cox

What Every Student Should Know About Researching Online (0-321-44531-7)
David Munger / Shireen Campbell

What Every Student Should Know About Citing Sources with APA Documentation (0-205-49923-6)
Chalon E. Anderson / Amy T. Carrell / Jimmy L. Widdifield, Jr.

What Every Student Should Know About Citing Sources with MLA Documentation (0-321-44737-9)
Michael Greer

What Every Student Should Know About Avoiding Plagiarism (0-321-44689-5)
Linda Stern

What Every Student Should Know About Peer Review (0-321-44848-0)
Michelle Trim

Multimedia Offerings

MyWritingLab (www.mywritinglab.com)
MyWritingLab is a complete online learning system with *better* practice exercises to make students better writers. The exercises in MyWritingLab are progressive, which means within each skill module students move from literal comprehension to critical application to demonstrating their skills in their own writing. The 9,000+ exercises in the system do rehearse grammar, but they also extend into the writing process, paragraph development, essay development, and research. A thorough diagnostic test outlines where student have not yet mastered the skill, and an easy-to-use tracking systems enables students and instructors to monitor all work in MyWritingLab.

STATE SPECIFIC SUPPLEMENTS

For Florida Adopters:
Thinking Through the Test: A Study Guide for the Florida College Basic Skills Exit Test, by D.J. Henry and Mimi Markus

FOR FLORIDA ADOPTIONS ONLY. This workbook helps students strengthen their reading skills in preparation for the Florida College Basic Skills Exit Test. It features both diagnostic tests to help assess areas that may need improvement and exit tests to help test skill mastery. Detailed explanatory answers have been provided for almost all of the questions. *Package item only—not available for sale.* Available Versions:

Available Versions:	
Thinking Through the Test A Study Guide for the Florida College Basic Skills Exit Tests: Reading and Writing, without Answers 3/e	0-321-38740-6
Thinking Through the Test A Study Guide for the Florida College Basic Skills Exit Tests: Reading and Writing, with Answers, 3/e	0-321-38739-2
Thinking Through the Test A Study Guide for the Florida College Basic Skills Exit Tests: Writing, with Answers, 3/e	0-321-38741-4
Thinking Through the Test A Study Guide for the Florida College Basic Skills Exit Tests: Writing, without Answers, 3/e	0-321-38934-4

Preparing for the CLAST, 7/e by H. Ramsay Fowler (Instructor/Print ISBN 0-321-01950-4)
These two, 40-item objective tests evaluate students' readiness for the Florida CLAST exams. Strategies for teaching CLAST preparedness are included.

For Texas Adopters
The Pearson THEA Study Guide, by Jeannette Harris (Student/ 0-321-27240-4)
Created specifically for students in Texas, this study guide includes straightforward explanations and numerous practice exercises to help students prepare for the reading and writing sections of THEA Test. *Package item only—not available for sale.*

For New York/CUNY Adopters
Preparing for the CUNY-ACT Reading and Writing Test, edited by Patricia Licklider (Student/ 0-321-19608-2)
This booklet, prepared by reading and writing faculty from across the CUNY system, is designed to help students prepare for the CUNY-ACT exit test. It includes test-taking tips, reading passages, typical exam questions, and sample writing prompts to help students become familiar with each portion of the test.

Instructor Supplements

Pearson is pleased to offer a variety of support materials to help make teaching developmental English easier on teachers and to help students excel in their coursework. Many of our student supplements are available free or at a greatly reduced price when packaged with a Pearson writing textbook. Contact your local Pearson sales representative for more information on pricing and how to create a package.

On the Front Lines by Donna Bontatibus (0-205-81680-0)
On the Front Lines is a practical, streamlined guide designed for the instructors—new, adjunct, temporary, and even seasoned—of developmental writing at the community college. Within eight concise chapters, instructors receive realistic, easy-to-apply advice that centers on the preparation and teaching of developmental writing in a nation with over 1,000 community colleges. Instructors will be walked through the process of preparing a syllabus; structuring the classroom experience; appealing to different learning styles; teaching with technology; constructing and evaluating assignments; and conferencing with students. This accessible guide also encourages instructors to look outside the classroom-- to familiarize themselves with campus resources and policies that support the classroom experience--and to look ahead for their own professional development opportunities. Given the debates on developmental education and the importance of first-year experience initiatives to assist with student transition and retention, there is a monumental amount of weight placed on the shoulders of instructors of developmental writing. *On the Front Lines* respects the instructor's role in the developmental writing

classroom and offers practical, straightforward guidance to see the instructor through the preparation of classes to the submission of final grades.

The Pearson Developmental Writing PowerPoints (0-205-75219-5)
To complement face-to-face and online courses, The Pearson Developmental Writing PowerPoint resource provides overviews on all the elements of writing an effective essay. This pedagogically sound PowerPoint guide will provide instructors and students with informative slides on writing patterns – classification, cause/effect, argument, etc. – and common grammatical errors, with questions and answers included.

The Pearson Test Bank for Developmental Writing (Print Version) by Janice Okoomian with contributions by Mimi Markus—available via the Instructor Resource Center ONLY (0-321-08486-1)
This test bank features more than 5,000 questions in all areas of writing. In addition to extensive grammar practice, the test bank covers paragraphs and essays, including such topics as the writing process and documentation. Instructors simply log on to the Instructor Resource Center (IRC) to download and print the tests of their choice.

MyTest for The Pearson Test Bank for Developmental Writing (online only) (0-205-79834-9)
This test bank features more than 5,000 questions in all areas of writing, from grammar to paragraphing through essay writing, research, and documentation. Through this instructor friendly program instructors are able to edit these questions and tests to suit their classroom needs and are also allowed more flexibility to manage assessments at any time.

Diagnostic and Editing Tests with Exercises, 9/e (0-321-41524-8)
This collection of diagnostic tests helps instructors assess students' competence in standard written English to determine placement or to gauge progress.

The Pearson Guide to Community Service-Learning in the English Classroom and Beyond by Elizabeth Rodriguez Kessler (0-321-12749-8)
Written by Elizabeth Rodriguez Kessler of University of Houston, this monograph provides a definition and history of service-learning, as well as an overview of how service-learning can be integrated effectively into the college classroom.

Instructor Resource Center

Getting Registered

To register for the Instructor Resource Center, go to www.pearsonhighered.com.

1. Click **"Educators"**; the first picture on the left.
2. Click **"Instructor Resource Center"** on the top navigation.
3. Request access to download digital supplements by clicking the **"Register"** button.

Follow the provided instructions. Once you have been verified as a valid Pearson instructor, an instructor code will be emailed to you. Please use this code to set up your Pearson login name and password. After you have set up your username and password, proceed to the directions below.

Downloading Resources

1. Go to www.pearsonhighered.com and use the "Search Our Catalog" option to find your text. You may search by Author, Title, or ISBN.

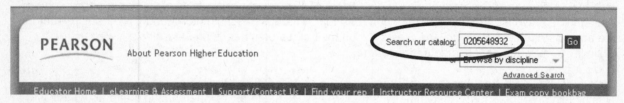

----

2. **Select your text** from the provided results.

----

3. After being directed to the catalog page for your text, click the **Instructor** link located under **Resources**.

Clicking the Instructor link will provide a list of all of the book-specific print and digital resources for your text below the main title. Items available for download will have a icon.

----

4. **Click the highlighted file name** of the version you want to download.

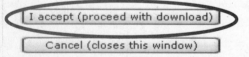 Instructor's Manual (1.2MB | zip file | Type: Manuals/Guides)

You will be prompted to login with an Instructor Resource Center login.

----

5. Enter your login name & password, and click the **"Log In"** button.

----

6. Read the terms and conditions and then click the **"I accept"** button to begin the download process.

    I accept (proceed with download)

    Cancel (closes this window)

----

7. **"Save"** the supplement file to a folder you can easily find again.

Once you are signed into the IRC, you may continue to download additional resources from our online catalog.

Please "Sign Out" when you are finished.

CHAPTER 1

Developmental English: You Have Chosen to Accept this Writing Assignment

Objectives:

- *To learn about the students for whom the community college serves*

- *To understand the historical context of developmental English*

- *To review key terms associated with developmental education*

Congratulations! You have been offered the assignment to teach part time as a developmental English adjunct in one—maybe even more than one—of the nation's 1,177 community colleges (American Association of Community Colleges "Fast Facts"). In fact, you will be part of the over 60 percent of college faculty who teach part time at community colleges (Marti 44). Even more, you will be part of the 65 percent of faculty who teach developmental courses part time at a community college (Boylan 55).

Without a doubt, your assignment is certainly of great academic importance: You will be teaching one—maybe two, maybe even three—courses in developmental English in a nation where approximately 65 percent of first-time students attending community college will need to take at least one remedial or precollege level course (Roueche 19). Generally, most college students will be required to take a composition course or two as part of their curricula or programs of study to graduate. However, there are many students who need the additional support with reading, writing, and perhaps even study skills before assuming the challenge of the required ENG101 Composition course.

And this is why your teaching assignment in developmental English is so far reaching: You are providing prospective students—over a million students each year enroll in a remedial or developmental course according to Robert H. McCabe in *Yes We Can!*—the opportunity to develop the writing and reading skills so necessary to be successful in college. Ideally, the skills acquired in your developmental writing course will not only assist students in their college-level English courses but also their general education and discipline-specific courses as they progress

1

with their curricula. Indeed, as an adjunct instructor of developmental writing, you are pivotally placed on the front lines of your students' college educations. If anyone can make a profound difference in the academic lives of your students, it will be you.

However, your writing assignment does bear its challenges. While over a million students each year enroll in at least one remedial course, approximately 25 percent of students drop out (McCabe 45). Much of the literature about first-year students, particularly those needing developmental courses, insist that within the first six months of college life, students will decide whether or not to return. Nearly half of first-year students make the decision not to return for the second year (McCabe 60).

Community College Students

With these startling statistics, then, who are the students attending community colleges today? The community college opens its doors to diverse populations. According to the Association of Community Colleges, nearly half of our nation's undergraduates attend community colleges. To be a bit more specific, approximately 11.7 million students are attending community colleges: 5 million on the noncredit side and 6.7 million for credit. With regard to gender, 58 percent are women, and 42 percent are men. Of the students who attend community colleges, 39 percent are the first generation of their families (American Association of Community Colleges "Fast Facts").

Why do students opt to attend community colleges? The open access provides workforce development, job training, English as Second Language offerings, skill development, certificate and/or Associate Degree obtainment, personal enrichment, and transfer to four-year colleges or universities. In fact, the national transfer rate is estimated at approximately 25 percent. However, community colleges also experience what has been dubbed "'reverse transfer'"— movement by students from a four-year institution to a two-year college (Lester 47). Demographically, though, the average age of a community college student is 29, with 40 percent of students holding full-time jobs, and 60 percent holding part-time jobs. With more geographic and financial accessibility, the community college provides a diversity of individuals an opportunity to further their education (American Association of Community Colleges "Fast Facts").

Not surprisingly with the rising costs of tuition and the competitive element of private colleges and public universities, 40 percent of our nation's undergraduates are opting to be first-time freshman in community colleges. To get a clearer sense of the diverse landscape of the community college, community college students reflect the following percentages of undergraduates in the nation: 52 percent Native American; 43 percent Black; 45 percent Asian Pacific Islander; and 52 percent Hispanic (American Association of Community Colleges "Fast Facts"). With regard to access, the community college truly lives the message of "The New Colossus," the prolific sonnet penned by Emma Lazarus. It's a fascinating connection—our nation's first free-standing community college opened its doors in 1902, and "The New Colossus" was proudly attached to the pedestal of the Statue of Liberty in 1903.

Brief History

The need, however, for preparatory, remedial, or developmental courses is not new; in fact, this need predates 1902 and the community college. Developmental education finds its roots in a curious history, notwithstanding its controversy. In brief, there are many social, political, and historical factors that influence how precollege courses are defined or determined beyond admission standards within a college or university in a given decade of a century. Yes, century. In fact, in America, this need for precollege assistance dates back to the 1600s. In "Then and Now: The Early Years of Developmental Education," David R. Arendale traces the different phases of developmental education, with the earliest phase being from mid-1600s to the 1820s. During this early phase, tutors at Harvard (established in 1636, Harvard claims the first to offer remediation) and Yale (established in 1701) were needed to prepare their all-male—oftentimes clergy-bound—students to take their entrance examinations in Greek and Latin (Arendale 7). The academic landscape of education, though, was bound for expansion beyond the walls of the ivy league and beyond courses in Greek and Latin.

Over time, with the mission and purpose of education evolving throughout the nineteenth century to reach more people in a democratic society, remediation included other subjects. Cited as the first, or one of the first, universities to systematize precollege assistance, the University of Wisconsin formed the Department of Preparatory Studies in 1849. In this department, students could gain assistance in study skills, arithmetic, reading, and writing. Interestingly, more than half of the enrolled students at the university needed at least one course in preparatory studies (Arendale 10). Over in New England, authors Charles Townsend Copeland and Henry Milner Rideout, in their book *Freshman English and Theme Correcting* (1901), bemoan the challenges

3

posed by the approximately 630 Harvard students in English A, freshman-level composition (1899–1900) to their 11 instructors. Copeland and Rideout explain that

> …the habitual use of correct and intelligent English, is what the instructors try to drill into the Freshman. The problem is not without its difficulties. At one extreme of this class of Freshman are the illiterate and inarticulate, who cannot distinguish a sentence from a phrase, or spell the simplest words. At the other are fairly mature writer, who need only to discard certain crudities and to gain variety and flexibility. Between these two extremes come many sorts and conditions of students. (Copeland 2)

For their audience, Copeland and Rideout do classify the specific challenges—i.e., spelling and sentence identification—faced by the Harvard freshman who needed some basic instruction in English. Even more, the authors document the challenges confronted by instructors who are teaching large numbers of students within a class where the range in skill level is quite broad. Indeed, Harvard and the University of Wisconsin held two different pedagogical approaches to students' skill development—basic approaches still existent today.

The need, though, for precollege level courses persisted throughout the twentieth century. With the assistance of federal legislation, the doors of colleges and universities, though barriers still certainly existed, began to open to more and more people. By the early 1900s, junior colleges (now called community colleges) began to populate the United States. Established in 1902, Joliet Junior College is considered the first "free-standing" community college, while the University of Chicago has been credited with offering a junior college within its university in 1892 (Arendale 14). Throughout the twentieth century, the number of community colleges grew, as did the offerings in precollege, preparatory, or remedial coursework.

As the number of community colleges expanded with their mission reaching more and more of the populace, the controversy surrounding where to house remedial or developmental education classes intensified. Oftentimes, the debate centered on whether or not remediation should be concentrated in just the community colleges or should be shared by four-year colleges and universities. By the 1980s, the concept of developmental education (a more comprehensive approach to educating students by building from their strengths to address underdeveloped skill areas) rather than remediation (a fragmented approach to education that works from a more deficient correction model) firmly emerged, with community colleges becoming the primary providers of developmental education for the nation's undergraduates.

Today, developmental English courses may be part of an English department or a humanities division, which oversees all the English courses from developmental to advanced writing or literature. On the other hand, the courses themselves may be housed in a separate developmental studies division along with developmental mathematics, study skills, and support services. Essentially, the home of developmental writing within a given community college does vary across the nation.

The Need for Developmental Writing

Affordability, increasing enrollments, and the expanding demographics—the need for developmental education is greater than ever, and, indeed, the nation entrusts the community colleges with meeting this need. However, the necessity for writing instruction appears unparalleled, and calls to provide more intense instruction are being directed to the nation's middle and high schools. In a policy brief entitled "Making Writing Instruction a Priority in America's Middle and High Schools," the Alliance for Excellent Education asks the nation to improve writing instruction in middle and high schools because "the stakes are far higher today than at any time in the nation's history" (1). The report goes on to argue that the traditional high school graduates of the nineteenth and twentieth centuries "couldn't have dreamed of a world as saturated with writing as now exists, both in the workplace and in private life. The majority of American employers now consider writing proficiency to be an essential skill that is becoming ever more critical as the information-based economy continues to expand" (Alliance for Excellent Education 1). The Alliance for Excellent Education emphasizes that writing proficiency permeates many sectors of the American workforce, including technical, clerical, and support positions (1). Interestingly, the report further acknowledges that "college instructors estimate about 50 percent of high school graduates are unprepared for college-level writing" (1). Indeed, the nation's community colleges are charged unofficially and officially (e.g., Florida) with the delivery of developmental education, which includes English; however, the emphasis on writing skill development, as noted by the Alliance for Excellent Education, needs to predate a student's entrance into a community college.

Developmental English—Writing and Reading

Generally, developmental English involves writing and reading, and the ways that the courses are structured vary across the nation's community colleges. Some colleges offer more area-specific courses where writing and reading are treated as separate courses (not that the two can truly be separated) and may even be multileveled. Other colleges may have more formally combined reading and writing courses that may appear in three-, four- or even six-credit structures. Some college may offer one level of developmental writing and reading, and others may offer two or three levels of both writing and reading. Regarding content, the lowest levels of developmental writing may focus on sentence to paragraph with an emphasis on grammar and punctuation. The more intermediate levels of developmental writing may focus on paragraph to essay framed around the rhetorical modes (narration, description, process, cause-effect, comparison-contrast, etc.), though any level of writing, including composition, may include discussions of the rhetorical modes. Moving sequentially, the upper end of the developmental writing courses may be structured as more of a bridge to college composition. Within these upper-level developmental writing courses, the essay's focus may include more reader response and/or opinion-support along with basic documentation. It is not unusual for a bridge course to have both a reader and writing guide if the two texts are not combined into one. Like writing, reading may be multileveled, with the more foundational levels of reading focusing on reading strategies, main idea and supporting detail identification. Intermediate reading levels may teach reading strategies that are more discipline or genre specific as students will experience difference subjects across their curricula. Essentially, there is a range of developmental writing and reading courses, and the focus of each certainly may vary by institutional need.

Placement Testing

Overall, the level of writing and reading for each student is determined by placement testing. Some colleges and states actually may have their own assessment tools (e.g., standardized tests, essays), while other colleges may rely on more nationally available testing instruments, such as Compass, Asset, or Accuplacer, to identify students' reading comprehension, sentence skills, or essay writing levels for placement. Even more, colleges may utilize different combinations of assessment, including the use of SAT or ACT scores, to determine writing and reading placements. Because each college—and state—is different, it's worth inquiring about how placement testing is performed on your campus. More than likely, your students took a placement test to claim seats in your classroom.

Credit versus Noncredit

Whether or not your developmental English course is credit-bearing varies from community college to community college. Some colleges do, in fact, offer zero credit because the credit cannot be utilized in programs of study or toward graduation. In other colleges, developmental courses may be three credits, four credits, or even six credits; however, the credit does not typically count toward students' programs of study, transfer, or graduation. As a result, developmental English, like other developmental courses, may be viewed as noncredit. The credit, though, may be tallied as part of the grade point average (GPA) or may even be linked to the eligibility to obtain financial aid. The lack of graduation course credit per se can be quite discouraging to students; however, it is important for students to realize that developmental English serves as the vital prerequisite for college composition. More concretely, developmental English will provide students the necessary skill sets in sentence construction, paragraph development, essay formation, editing, and proofing—the foundation for students to write unified, coherent, thoughtful compositions across the curriculum.

The developmental writing course, as many instructors learn, offers so much more to students. According to Alexander W. Astin in *What Matters in College*, English writing courses and other courses that include writing potentially sharpen students' skills in critical thinking, public speaking, interpersonal communication, and even leadership. In essence, the tangible and intangible lessons learned in developmental writing have the potential of being far reaching in students' lives personally, academically, and professionally.

An overview of developmental English as it's situated within developmental education may not appear directly related to your teaching assignment of developmental writing. However, what this context does offer is the understanding that your developmental writing course is part of a history. If you understand the context of developmental English and its organizational structures, hopefully your teaching will be especially informed and your dedication strengthened even more—as you are placed on the front lines of your students' college educations.

Defining Key Terms

While teaching developmental English at the community college, you may, in fact, encounter several terms denoting your area and classifying your students. Some of the more common terms include the following.

At-risk

Unlike the term ***underprepared*** (see p. 10), ***at-risk*** characterizes students who may or may not need developmental-level coursework. ***At risk*** describes students whose realities—albeit personal, academic, financial, familial, work related—put them at increased risk for not completing college. First-generation-to-attend college students and students who reflect the average age (29 years) of today's community college population are also considered at risk (Roueche 18).

Developmental Education

According to The National Association for Developmental Education (NADE), developmental education "is a comprehensive process that focuses on the intellectual, social and emotional growth and development of all students. Developmental education includes, but is not limited to, tutoring, personal/career counseling, academic advisement, and coursework" ("2009 Fact Sheet" 1). In developmental education, the coursework primarily centers upon writing, reading, mathematics, and study skills. In some colleges, the developmental-level courses may be offered in the sciences, social sciences, business, and other discipline-specific subjects, as well.

High-risk Courses

If courses produce 30 percent or more final grades of D and F, and/or withdrawals, the courses themselves are considered "high risk" (Pascarella 106).

Nontraditional

Generally, the term *nontraditional* applies to students who delay attending college for various reasons and is usually defined as 25 years or older. However, nontraditional may also characterize students who enroll part time; hold full-time employment; have dependents; or who are single parents (Compton 73). At the community college, more than likely you will have both the nontraditional and traditional (those who generally attend college after completing high school) students in your class.

Remedial and Developmental

Over the last decade or two, several terms—remedial, preparatory, basic skills, developmental—have evolved to identify students who need precollege-level skill development in writing, reading, and mathematics. In many cases, the different terms are used interchangeably, but each does have its own historical context. Generally, the term ***developmental*** is used "to describe instruction that prepares students for specific college courses or programs (e.g., studying effectively, thinking critically), and ***remedial*** is used to describe instruction that has or should have been provided in the past (e.g., reading, math, writing)" (Roueche vii-viii). In sum, the term remedial is grounded in the context of skill-deficiency correction, and the term developmental emerged from "more complex, organized efforts to develop the cognitive and affective talents that describe the whole student" (Roueche viii). The developmental approach (emerging from the late 1970s, early 1980s) works from the assumption that students have strengths, and these strengths can be utilized in the process of building students' underdeveloped areas. Again, both terms tend to be used interchangeably, but their historical contexts and approaches to student development do differ (Casazza 31).

Retention

Generally, retention deals with an institution's ability to retain students to their next semester, their next academic year—the time it takes to graduate and/or transfer to a four-year institution. Indeed, many states and their community colleges are struggling with the reality of increasing enrollment in developmental courses and the fledgling retention. To address the challenge of retention, many colleges are exploring, assessing, and implementing campus-wide initiatives, such as extended orientations, intensive advising, self-paced courses, college success courses, learning communities, and early warning/notification systems to support their first-semester students. Over the last thirty years, increased emphasis has been placed on the first year of college—the importance of helping students transition to college and ultimately persist to their next year. For students who take developmental courses, the transition period is crucial. While over a million students each year enroll in at least one remedial course, approximately 25 percent of students drop out (McCabe 45). With the many retention-driven initiatives to help students adjust to college, there is one element in study after study that proves imperative in helping students persist: the instructor-student relationship.

Underprepared

Underprepared is another term used to classify college students who are not quite ready to meet the challenge of college-level work. While the course numbering systems vary at community colleges across the nation, generally, course numbers in English with 101 and higher are considered college level (Roueche 5).

Helpful Hints

- Learn more about your developmental writing assignment by browsing through the college catalog or by visiting your online catalog located on your college's Web site. Review the course description to your course as well as the other developmental courses to understand the sequence in reading and writing.

- Review your college's developmental English sequence. As an instructor, it's important that your students understand where the course fits into the sequence. For advising purposes, your students may need to know if they have to take another developmental writing course next semester, or, whether or not, their next stop is Composition 101. If you have questions about the developmental English sequences at your college, ask your department chair or coordinator for more information. You may even refer your students to their academic advisors or an academic advisement center if they have any questions about their English requirements.

- Inquire about the method of placement testing on your campus because more than likely your students took some form of assessment to place in your class.

- Locate your college's mission statement to see how your college—your teaching—connects with the community. Oftentimes, the mission statement will be located in your college catalog or on the college Web site.

CHAPTER 2

Preparing for Class

Objectives:

- *To learn about what questions to ask*

- *To review the components of a syllabus*

- *To understand the importance of campus resources*

Asking Questions or Inquiring About the Developmental English Course Assignment

Whether you are a new adjunct of developmental English or a veteran, it is important to ask informed questions about your course assignment and request course-related materials, especially for a course that you have not taught before. Each college, particularly when size becomes a factor, has its own way of preparing or "prepping"—or maybe not prepping— adjuncts for the classroom experience. On the one hand, colleges may offer a fairly comprehensive preparation. As part of a mini-orientation, you may initially meet with your chair to review your course assignment or to discuss departmental guidelines. You may even be provided informative, handy packets or manuals (electronic or hard copy) of relevant materials, but even with the most comprehensive prep, there are elements of which you must be mindful. On the other hand, particularly when colleges are faced with limited human and financial resources or simply when colleges hold a more instructor-is-responsible perspective, adjuncts need to assume more responsibility in seeking out the information to initiate course prep. Regardless of whether or not you receive some orientation by a college administrator or faculty member, one lesson prevails: You need to take a more active rather than passive role in obtaining the information to prep for a course. To assume a more active role on the front lines of your students' educations, ask questions and seek out relevant course-related information. Where then to start?

The Basics

When you receive the initial assignment, you may be given the course number, the time, location, and even the section number. If you are not provided the specifics about the course number or section, ask your department or division chair or secretary for clarification. Even the course schedules (print or online at the college's Web site) for fall, spring, and summer may be consulted for basic course identification. Many colleges have the course schedules in print and online. With developmental English, there may be many sections of Introduction to Writing, Introduction to the Essay, Academic Writing, and the many other names titling a developmental-level writing course. Usually, the course name, number, and section will be accompanied by the room location, which is also quite handy, because you can visit the classroom in advance to review layout and the availability of technology. Indeed, course prep begins with the basics.

Texts and Instructional Supplements

Once you know the course assignment, you need to inquire about the course text and support materials. Essentially, each college has its own timetable with regard to staffing, course prep, and text distribution because the staffing process consumes a considerable amount of time. In some departments, there may be a common text used for all sections of a particular course. Depending on the department's procedures, you may be provided a copy or be directed to obtain one yourself. If you do not know whether or not a text will be provided at some point, you need to ask for one or learn how to obtain a copy.

In other instances, you may have an opportunity to select your text from several that the department endorses. If this is the case, review each text carefully. To help with the decision process, review the course description and objectives/outcomes (ask your chair or the department secretary for this information if it has not already been provided) to help identify the text for you. If you need more assistance with the decision process, ask your chair for some feedback or ask your chair to identify a faculty member who could provide some feedback. In the market, there are many multileveled developmental writing texts, and it is important that you have the text that reflects your teaching style and, most importantly, allows you to meet the course outcomes.

In general, there tends to be three primary foci with developmental writing texts: (1) the foundation levels will focus on sentence to paragraph, (2) a more intermediate range will focus on paragraph to essay, and (3) the top of the range tends to focus primarily on the essay. The latter is often utilized as a bridge to the traditional college-level composition course. Many developmental writing texts organize the essay around the rhetorical modes (narrative, description, process, comparison-contrast, cause-effect, and argument) once the basic four- or five-paragraph model is addressed. Other texts may concentrate on more of an opinion-support essay format organized by themes or topics, such as media, family, culture, education, and technology. To expand the options even more, the different texts may integrate varying degrees of reading selections, grammar, punctuation, and mechanics. For those that are closer to the college composition end of the spectrum, some texts will include response-to-reading essay organizational formats accompanied by basic MLA citation and Works Cited reviews. For courses that integrate a significant amount of developmental reading, there are abbreviated anthologies or developmental readers that are organized by rhetorical mode and/or theme. Oftentimes, these texts may include study skills and reading comprehension reviews to help students become more skilled in genre analysis. All in all, the course description and outcomes (what the students need to have learned by the end of the semester) will assist in determining the appropriate course text if this decision is placed in your hands.

Still, in other cases, you may be solely responsible for the text selection. If this is the situation and you are not familiar with how to access texts from different publishers and submit book orders, ask for some initial assistance. The chair or a representative from the department may have some exam copies of texts for you to review. If not, ask for some publisher names and visit their Web sites. Publishers have sections on their sites specifically for instructors, so instructors can review different texts and request exam copies. Additionally, publishers provide support materials, such as instructor's manuals, text-quiz banks, electronic classroom presentation materials (PowerPoint slides), and other online access to instructional databases. Once you know the publisher of your text, go online to order a copy—if you haven't already—along with the instructor supplements. If you are responsible for selecting your course, you may also be responsible for filling out and submitting a book order for your class. Be sure to ask your chair or division secretary for the appropriate procedure. While there may be no perfect text, the text that you select needs to assist you in delivering course outcomes and fulfilling course requirements.

Course Requirements

Developmental English, writing courses in particular, may have specific course requirements. These requirements may be presented to you when you receive your course assignment or sometime thereafter. The requirements might identify the minimum number of essays, specific organizational formats preferred (rhetorical modes, opinion-support only, reader or literary response), minimum number of words for specific types of essay assignments, or even if the course is portfolio based.

Portfolios, in fact, are a staple of developmental writing courses. Essentially, students may be asked to collect a body of their writing in a portfolio that will be assessed at the end of the term, or even earlier, depending on a department's purpose and policy for portfolio evaluation. Portfolios are usually used when a department or instructor prefers more holistic assessment in which a significant portion of a student's final grade is determined by a range of the student's work, which also charts writing progress throughout the semester. Portfolio guidelines for purpose, content, and assessment vary from department to department for those colleges that choose to utilize more of a portfolio-based developmental writing course (more information about writing portfolios will be discussed in chapter 5). If specific course content requirements are not brought to your attention, ask if there are any course guidelines. If the guidelines tend to be more individualized by instructors within a department, ask for some samples. The samples may help you make informed decisions about how to approach the assignment of essays and ultimately the review of the writing process in your class. In sum, whether course guidelines are departmental, individualized by instructor, or even a combination of both the department and instructor, your consideration of these areas will assist in the formation of your course syllabus provided to students the first day or week of the semester.

The Course Syllabus: Content

Basically, the syllabus provides an overview of the course and perhaps even a course outline of weekly assignments and readings. In many cases, you may be required by your department and/or community college to compile a syllabus to distribute to your students the first day or week of class. In fact, some departments and colleges may have specific contract requirements that identify the categories (e.g., course description, outcomes, etc.) that need to be included within a syllabus. To be safe, if you need a sample syllabus, ask your chair or the department secretary for a copy. Sample syllabi will allow you to glean the important features of the course, the course work, and even the particular chapters reviewed from a text—all to assist in the preparation of your own syllabus.

Course Identification

One basic element of a syllabus is the course information. This would include course name, course number, section number, room location, class day and time, credit/noncredit status, and any other course identification information provided by your college. Oftentimes, the college's fall, spring, or summer course schedules—print and online—will have this information.

Contact Information

Another component is your contact information. Be sure that your information is clearly stated, usually at the beginning of the syllabus, because your students need to know your method of out-of-class communication. Include your preferred title of address and your preferred method of contact. Your method of contact may be individualized, or the college may provide you with an e-mail address or even access to a course management system, such as Blackboard, where course-by-course e-mail may be transacted. If you have access to a college voicemail system, then you certainly can provide the extension number. Unless there is a recommendation or requirement by your department or college, the method of contact with students tends to be individualized. Lastly, colleges may require that you keep office hours. Typically, the college will define the number of minutes, if any, that you may be required or recommended to be available for your students each week.

However, one significant challenge faced by many adjuncts is the lack of office space and the necessary equipment, such as phones and computers, to conduct your office hours. In many colleges, even the full-time staff and faculty struggle to find appropriate space and resources, but do inquire about office space at your college. If the space is available, more than likely, it will be shared with other instructors. To address the lack of appropriate space, some adjuncts seek alternative, unfortunately less-than-ideal, solutions. Some may hold office hours in the classroom just before or after class, if the room is available; others may find a space in the library, cafeteria, or any spot that appears viable to cope with the office space limitations. Once you determine where you can hold office hours, identify the location in the syllabus.

Required Texts and Course Materials

In the syllabus, identify the title of the course text(s), the edition, and the publisher information, as well. With the availability of online resources, students need the appropriate information for purchase. Actually, if you have any specific supply requirements, such as journals or pocket portfolio folders, let your students know early on, even if you opt not to mention the specific supplies in the syllabus.

Course Description and Course Outcomes

In addition, the syllabus includes the course description and outcomes. Especially with the increased emphasis on assessment, the description and outcomes tend to be standard components. The course description can be readily obtained from course catalogs (print or online) or sample syllabi. When you review the course description with your students, explain how your particular writing course may be situated in the sequence of developmental writing. Ultimately, developmental writing serves as the prerequisite for college composition. As a prerequisite, developmental writing may, in fact, strengthen students' abilities to perform well at the next level of writing and within any course that requires writing for reports, tests, or projects. Although some students will be severely disappointed about having been placed in a developmental sequence, emphasize that by fulfilling the course outcomes within the short term, they will strengthen their skills for the long term.

Indeed, course or learning outcomes are an important component of the syllabus. Without an extensive explanation on assessment, outcomes, in brief, are what students will learn by the end of the semester. Specifically, the course outcomes tell students what skills the coursework will help them achieve by the semester's end. However, the course outcomes also give the instructor direction. If one outcome is for students to learn essay organization formats, then the class lessons will include a review and practice of different essay formats. In essence, the learning outcomes provide valuable information for the students—and their instructors.

Policies and Procedures

In sum, the syllabus provides students an overview of the course, and, indeed, course policies and procedures (college-wide, departmental, and instructor specific) claim a portion of this overview. Policies and procedures may encompass many areas, including attendance, classroom etiquette, grading (especially how the final grade is formulated), and even essay format requirements. On a college-wide level, the syllabus may need to include specific information regarding academic honesty or plagiarism. Even more, the syllabus may need to reference the Americans with Disabilities Act (ADA) and other vital support services (acknowledging that the college provides these services and identifying the office or point person for additional contact.) With college-wide policies and procedures, it's important to understand what you can and cannot do or say. If you are provided sample syllabi, plagiarism statements and disability support service identification may be present for you to review in advance of your own syllabus preparation. In addition, the college catalog serves as an important source of policies and procedures. Albeit directly or indirectly, the policies and procedures outlined in the college catalog do connect with instruction and the classroom environment. Still in other instances, you may be provided information about college-wide or departmental policies or procedures at orientations for adjunct faculty. For the information alone, the orientations are important to attend.

In addition to acknowledging the more college-wide policies, your syllabus will reflect your own policies and procedures as well as those outlined by your department or division. In many cases, especially for developmental writing, departments or divisions may have specific requirements for assessing and passing students' writing. It is especially important, then, to inquire about grading. Regarding final grades, some departments may have minimum passing grade requirements; in other words, in order to pass a particular developmental writing course, a student needs to achieve a minimum grade of C or C-. Still, there may be departmental policies

17

that require students to receive a minimum grade of C or C- on an essay-based portfolio or final exam essay in order to be eligible to pass the course.

Each department's approach to final grade formation in developmental writing varies, as does each department's approach to handling grading student writing throughout the semester. Some may suggest, require, or recommend that you use the letter grade format. Other departments may suggest a check system (check-minus, check, check-plus) or point system with each check or number equating to a narrative assessment. The narrative may, then, address the quality of organization, thesis formation, development, transition use, critical analysis, grammar, or any area that is deemed relevant to the assignment and the course itself. All in all, this form of assessment assists students in the essay writing and/or revision process. In some cases, departments may have samples of narrative assessment to help instructors understand the process of assessing and progressing student writing. Overall, ask about how grading is handled in developmental writing, so you can apply accurate polices and relevant current practices. In some community colleges, departments offer professional development workshops to address grading, essay portfolios, teaching strategies, and other pedagogical topics.

In addition to grading procedures, the syllabus may identify policies and procedures that are specific to a class. Attendance statements sometimes may be individually determined; however, check to see if your department or college has any student attendance policies in place. If you have not formulated an attendance policy before and it falls completely within your purview to individualize, ask for samples from your department chair or other faculty members who are teaching the same course. Generally, attendance policies vary—everything from no policy to a minimum number of absences allowed. Sometimes, attendance is linked with classroom activity and participation grades. Some instructors may even implement policies regarding late arrivals and early departures. In the end, reviewing other current practices within the department will be helpful as you consider your own philosophy regarding attendance.

Along with attendance policies, your syllabus may also outline classroom etiquette—the do's and don'ts of acceptable classroom decorum. Remember, you are teaching a developmental writing course, so more than likely, many of your students may be first or second semester. During the first year, students are learning how to navigate appropriately within a college classroom environment. What might make the classroom environment more manageable? If you set the ground rules up front, you have at least established a foundation for a potentially smoother classroom experience. Though there may be specific college-wide policies in place, you can set additional standards by reminding students to arrive on time; to be prepared with books, notebooks, and assignments; to treat everyone respectfully, especially during discussions with controversial topics; and to turn off cell phones. If students are texting or reviewing cell phone messages, they are not learning. The latter policies may, in fact, come in handy during an exam. With one simple click, a student can send an exam question or answer to another student within the same class or in another section. Overall, classroom etiquette policies may potentially minimize disruptions for you and your students.

Another area to consider explaining within your syllabus is essay formats. If you have a certain way that you want papers formatted (double-spaced, word processed using a certain font size and typeface) and submitted (electronic copy or hard copy with pages stapled in a portfolio folder), let the students know the procedure. If there is a certain policy on late papers, the syllabus provides the space for the explanation. If there is a certain policy regarding the number of revisions, the syllabus provides the space to establish this requirement clearly, directly, and firmly. In essence, when creating a syllabus, instructors need to think in advance. Are there any standards and requirements (essay submission format, policy on late papers) that you would like to formulate and state in the syllabus? If there are certain standards that you would like to establish early to maintain classroom decorum, consider letting the syllabus present these important standards. Of course, unexpected challenges do arise. A savvy student, for example, may locate a loophole in your syllabus and confront you on it, especially if it impacts his or her grade. A repeatedly disruptive student in class, for example, may need more than a review of classroom etiquette. The student may need to be addressed by an administrator. In the end, clear statements of policy and procedure will encourage a safe, productive classroom experience; however, do seek immediate assistance from your chair, security, or the appropriate administrator if unexpected, unacceptable, or potentially harmful circumstances arise. Be aware of the policies and procedures that your college has in place in the event of an emergency.

Sometimes, there's just not enough time.

Realistically, there may be occasions when there is not enough time to prepare a course in advance. Department chairs handle many responsibilities, but one ever-present responsibility is

19

staffing, which is always in a state of flux. In any given semester, course enrollment can vary, which can cause courses, particularly multi-sectioned courses, to be dropped or added even as the new semester draws near. Just as course sections can be added or dropped, changes in staffing may take place, as well. In some cases, an instructor already assigned a course for the fall or spring semester may need later to decline the assignment, which leaves room for changes in course assignments at any point up through the start of a semester. What does this mean? Because of the nature of staffing and enrollment fluctuations, sometimes adjunct instructors can be assigned courses very close to the start of the new semester. While this may be extremely beneficial if you longed for a course to teach, it also leaves you little time to prepare for class. Even more importantly, ask questions before and after the semester starts to ensure that your teaching meets the department's course requirements and the students' academic needs.

The Syllabus as a Learning Tool

Indeed, the syllabus acts as the course "road map," giving direction and guidance until the ultimate destination is reached. As important as this map is to setting the pace and tone of the course, it is even more important as a learning tool. Sometimes, though, it might not have been referenced or reviewed after the first week or two of classes. Don't let students relegate the syllabus to the back of a pocket folder or notebook. Encourage students to form the habit of periodically reviewing their syllabus by actually role modeling this behavior by referencing the syllabus throughout the semester. Essentially, new students, particularly students who are at risk of dropping or opting out, need to learn skills or habits that will help them manage their college courses, including developmental writing. Thus, teaching your students how to read and use the syllabus may prove an invaluable learning experience for the short and long term.

How, then, can the syllabus be utilized within the class after the first week? If it includes a calendar or outline of daily or weekly activity, the syllabus can be more beneficial than you realize. To give the students direction at the start of class, have your students take out the calendar or outline section, so you or your students can review the focus of the class period. For example, in my courses—developmental and advanced—one of the first activities that I do in each class is to ask the students to take out the calendar portion of the course syllabus. After I review the basic objectives of the day's lesson, I will reference the syllabus because it indicates the reading assignment or the chapter under review. Even more, I can point out for my students the relationships among the different class lessons. *Today, we are reviewing how to write a thesis statement and supporting points from chapter 2. The next time we meet, we will review chapter 3, which will help us understand how to develop your essay with detailed support. These lessons will help you compose your first essay assignment, which is due September 10th.* This may be a simplistic example, but the point is that you are helping your students see the relationships— albeit quickly—between one lesson and the next. By noting the due date of the upcoming assignment, you are helping your students tap into their time management and goal-setting skills for planning. The syllabus can also be referenced at other points, especially if it outlines how you want your students to format or submit their essays. If students adopt the habit of reviewing their syllabi even out of class, they may, in fact, manage homework and their other assignments more efficiently to keep the pace of the course—maybe just enough to help them stay in class.

There is another way to utilize the syllabus as a learning tool. Indeed, different perspectives on syllabus formation exist. One theory is a more learner-centered one, in which instructors share some degree of power to construct the syllabus or even the types of activities experienced in class with their students. In *Learning-Centered Teaching*, Maryellen Weimer notes that this approach shifts the sole responsibility of course delivery away from the instructor and encourages students to assume more responsibility for their learning (xix). However, a learner-centered approach does not exclude policies or guidelines, especially for the new college student who may not be sure what to expect in or from a college classroom.

One example of applying a more learner-centered approach with a syllabus is to ask students to consider and contribute to appropriate components. In some cases, instructors ask their students to formulate some guidelines for classroom etiquette (e.g., no cell phone use) or suggestions on what students can do to be prepared for class (e.g., come with books, notebooks, homework assignments). In other cases, some instructors may ask the students to review and even select some readings that may be incorporated into class discussion. With some carefully constructed brainstorming activity or group work, you can guide your students to consider the conditions that would maximize learning.

There are, however, different degrees of student involvement in the creation of a more learner-centered syllabus. Again, consideration needs to be given to the fact that many students who place into developmental writing are new students who simply do not have a true understanding of the college classroom at the beginning of their academic journeys. The ultimate responsibility of the syllabus falls within the hands of the instructor to set the guidelines. If you would like to adopt a more learner-centered syllabus, Margaret Cohen, Barbara Millis, and Judith O'Brien, authors of *The Course Syllabus: A Learning-Centered Approach* have some suggestions. The syllabus may be used to

- Convey to your students what matters to you about learning.

- Set a tone for learning and how to learn that students will accept.

- Send a message about what students can expect from you and the campus community to support their learning during the term. (Cohen, Millis, O'Brien 11)

Indeed, the syllabus is an important document. In addition to providing relevant course information, the syllabus conveys attitudes toward learning, sets the tone for an environment conducive to learning, and demonstrates the college's commitment to students (Cohen, Millis, O'Brien 12). Ultimately, the syllabus invites students to accept responsibility for their share in the learning process.

Sample Syllabi Format

The list template on the following page summarizes the basic components of a syllabus. This list may serve as a foundation to build your own syllabus, including course-specific or college-specific policies and procedures.

Course Syllabus

Overview

- College Name

- Your Name and Preferred Title of Address

- Course Name, Number, Section, Credits (other related information)

- Course Room Number and Building

- Your Contact Information (e-mail and/or voicemail number)

- Office Hours and Location

- Course Description and/or Scope

- Course Text(s) and Materials

- Course Objectives/Outcomes (any related or similar material)

- Classroom Etiquette/ Expectations/Tips for Student Success

- Paper Format Guidelines

- Academic Honesty Statements, Plagiarism Policies

- Grading (outline of major assignments/overall worth in final grade/grading procedures). Some syllabi may even outline portfolio contents for a class that is portfolio based.

- Specific Support Service Identification (tutoring center or computer labs)

- Disability Service Identification

Course Calendar or Outline (daily, weekly, or monthly)

- Readings

- Major Assignment Due Dates

Knowing Campus Resources

Preparing a syllabus takes time and patience, especially for a new assignment. The preparation for class, though, does not end with the syllabus. To help prep for a teaching assignment, instructors need to familiarize themselves with the campus resources for instructors (e.g., e-mail, classroom technology, course management systems) and students (e.g., tutoring, career exploration). In many instances, college-wide adjunct orientations will provide some information, and materials may even be offered in a department-wide orientation. However, as comprehensive as the adjunct instructor prep may be within some colleges, you need to assume an active role in searching out the information to make your teaching assignment more manageable.

Campus Resources for Instructors

The availability of campus resources for adjunct instructors varies from college to college, but there are some basics for which you can inquire. College-wide e-mail may be one resource available. In addition to being a helpful form of communication with your chair, colleagues, and students, college e-mail access provides a window into campus life; some of this campus life, you may want to share with your students. For example, there may be a special art show, lecture, or literary event that you might encourage your students to attend. Maybe, you would like your students to write an essay interpreting a painting. With some advanced planning, this out-of-class activity (a visit to a campus art exhibit) can, then, become a co-curricular assignment, an assignment that links a class assignment (essay) and out-of-class activity. The options are numerous. On the other hand, you may receive an invitation to attend a professional development workshop at your college. Some adjuncts, though, may prefer to use their personal e-mail, which is understandable, but if your college offers a campus address, it would be beneficial to accept, even if only to benefit your students. You still may, if you chose, distribute your personal e-mails to students, but the addresses can be misplaced, or the students may not have the address with them when they need it the most. To be safe, have a backup.

College e-mail addresses generally share a similar format, one that students can access more readily from college Web sites. For many colleges, e-mail may be the most comprehensive way to communicate with significant numbers of adjunct instructors—to keep you informed, and, through you, your students.

In addition to e-mail, colleges may offer technological training. Depending on the college's resources, the range in training will vary. If you teach in a classroom that is considered technologically equipped with LCD players, computers, computer programs, etc., and you need some training, ask for a review, so you can function on the equipment effectively. Occasionally, technological failures or mishaps occur when setting up a lesson for class—I certainly have had my share and have occasionally helped a colleague in a bind. Needless to say, being prepared with a backup lesson plan comes in handy. Given your scheduling constraints, you might not attend every technological training session; however, keep your eyes open for the ones that may assist you with your class lessons—another good reason to use a campus e-mail address if your college offers one.

Course Management Systems and Platforms

More and more, colleges offer course-related systems or platforms to support distance learning and enhance ground courses. If, in fact, you have access to these educational technologies on your campus, explore them to determine how they would enhance your teaching. Whether your college provides Blackboard, Blackboard WebCT, Angel, Course Compass, eCollege, Sakai, or even ePortfolio (electronic portfolio systems), you may need to consider one-on-one or group training to ensure that you can technically function on these programs or platforms. Essentially, Blackboard, Blackboard Vista, etc., are platforms to facilitate online learning or distance learning courses. However, these platforms may also be provided by your college to supplement ground (traditional classroom-style) learning in that they can be an online file for students to access copies of your syllabus, notes, assignments, or any relevant materials to your course. These platforms also support threaded discussion (discussions in which students can respond to each other), chat, and blog opportunities for your students if you opt to utilize these features. Even more, the platforms contain e-mail access for not only you and your students to communicate but also for your students to communicate with each other. Additionally, your college may utilize an ePortfolio, which is a student-centered platform where your students can build an electronic portfolio of their work for and with you for assessment, showcasing, critical analysis, reflection, and more. With electronic portfolios, students can upload a variety of different materials in a centralized location of which you, and perhaps others if granted, have access. In some colleges, ePortfolio may be used in a developmental English classroom to help students compile a writing portfolio that will be used as an assessment tool for the course or even to facilitate a learning community (pairing or cluster of courses with the same cohort of students who come together for a shared learning experience). Regardless of the platform, if your college offers training, you need to consider attending, even if only to learn of the technological updates and new features.

In addition to the online platforms, publishers sell learning systems that can be utilized by students in and outside the classroom. For developmental English, learning systems, such as MyWritingLab, MyReadingLab, Catalyst, and others can be purchased packaged with a class text or separately from the text. These interactive systems are designed with many features, including video lessons, diagnostic assessment, and progressive exercises, that focus on the writing and reading processes. There are even developmental English classes housed in computer labs in which each student accesses a computer to work on course-related writing and reading activity. In these cases, the learning systems can be used to enhance a class lesson on thesis formation, transition use, organizational strategies, or even an element of grammar.

In other cases, these systems are adopted to facilitate self-paced learning. With self-paced learning, students work more independently with the learning systems, though they still may have instructor guidance. If the class is designed for more self-paced learning, assessments and progressive exercises can be tailored for each student. Even for developmental courses that do not include in-class access to computers, the learning systems provide out-of-class activities or homework for your students. The systems themselves are set up so you can be e-mailed or have access to your students' scores on the different assessments. Some systems even offer online tutorial support for students and plagiarism detection services for instructor use. The systems are much more than online quizzes and video explanations: They provide resources for both faculty and students. With the expansion of developmental education, self-paced learning will continue to grow throughout the country, possibly in an attempt to lessen some of the more academically driven attrition.

Resources for Students

As an instructor in developmental writing, you may encourage your students to seek tutorial support or other services that connect directly or indirectly with the classroom. For your students, conduct some research by reviewing the student service sections of the college catalog. Even visiting the college Web site to review the locations of the services will only take minutes. If there is English tutoring available at the writing center or learning center, let your students know in your syllabus by providing the name of the office or center (names vary) and the location. After all, you may be referring your students for tutoring in essay writing. To make academic tutoring more readily available to students who take both ground and online courses, some colleges may have eTutoring, a type of tutorial support which is conducted strictly online. Even some developmental writing textbooks with technological support may offer types of online tutoring. Before recommending the online academic tutoring services, learn more about them to see if they are appropriate to your students' needs.

In addition, if you want your students to word process their essays, list the location of a computer lab in your syllabus or let your students know that the responsibility falls upon them to locate the appropriate resources to fulfill your course or assignment requirements. Not all students own a personal computer or have word processing skills, so clearly define the expectations, even how to mechanically format an essay. In the end, you need to decide the extent of the academic services—tutorial or computer—that you want to identify on your syllabus or as a general announcement within class. You may even be of the school that the responsibility falls strictly upon the students to locate the services they need. Either way, be clear about your course and assignment expectations.

Moreover, there are some other students' services of which to be aware. Community colleges offer career counseling and Disability Support Services (DSS) for students. If you are conferencing with your student and your student reveals that he or she is struggling with a career choice, you can mention the career center at your college. However, for services that go beyond career, such as counseling and disability support, you need to know what is and what is not within your purview. College catalogs often provide general information about ADA and other services, or you may even receive an accommodation request for a student from disability support with some helpful insight. When more personal student services are involved, high

27

schools and community colleges differ in their approaches, so if you find yourself in need of additional information, seek out advice from college personnel in order to follow appropriate procedures.

If you are teaching developmental writing, why would knowing about student services be your responsibility? Or why go out of your way to find information for your syllabus when you weren't apprised about any requirements up front? Why even take the time out of your already busy schedule to take a workshop or two, especially when teaching, correcting essays, and conferencing with your students are time-consuming enough? Consider these challenges. Developmental writing is an essential course for students to progress to college composition and to other courses that have a composition prerequisite or corequisite. For students, developmental writing can be extremely demanding, and with some additional course features, such as minimum grades of C or C- to pass, the challenge intensifies for some students. Even more, developmental writing is considered a first- or second-semester course, and in light of the research conducted on the first year, students can potentially confront a variety of stresses that impact the classroom. Without a doubt, the instructor of developmental writing is on the front lines of these challenges—as these challenges converge for students in your classroom. In a reasonable relationship to your course, being equipped to help students, who are often considered high risk, transition to college is essential.

Helpful Hints

- Plan your syllabus carefully. Review sample syllabi and syllabus requirements set by your department or by the college.

- Visit your classroom in advance. With this visit, you can see firsthand the instructional tools—chalk board, whiteboard—available. You can also learn firsthand if the classroom has any technology. If there is technology and you think you may need some training, direct your inquiries to the appropriate office.

- Learn about the campus writing center or equivalent service where you may refer your students if they need tutoring.

- Consider obtaining a college e-mail address if one is available.

28

- Attend department or division workshops or campus-wide orientations for instructors. Many adjunct instructors may be teaching part time at other colleges or hold full-time employment at another institution, so they may not be able to attend workshops or orientations. However, it is important to make the commitment to learn about what your college offers in the workshops or orientations because the information will directly or indirectly affect the classroom experience for you and your students.

- Inquire about photocopying centers or machines that you need to access. Oftentimes, you will be responsible for submitting your syllabus and course materials for copy. Sometimes, you may have to submit these requests in advance to the college's copy center, or you may need to run your own copies on the department machine. Whether you utilize a copy center or run your own copies, inquire about procedures. Some colleges may set a limit or provide a code that you need to utilize when making copies.

CHAPTER 3

Teaching in Developmental Writing Classes

Objectives:

- *To review basic approaches to teaching Developmental Writing*

- *To learn about structuring the classroom experience*

- *To understand how to integrate college success skills*

From learning about campus resources to creating a syllabus, preparing to teach developmental writing is certainly an involved process. The preparation, though, does not stop with the syllabus: It also involves truly thinking through your role in the classroom. This thought process involves planning the actual delivery of the experience—how you would like to interact with your students and how you would like to frame the classroom activity to begin, sustain, and conclude the class.

Why is this thought process so important? Developmental writing is a pivotal course for students. Generally, through testing, students are placed into a developmental writing course. In some cases, colleges may have students engage in some form of self-placement through careful discussion with an advisor. Either way, when students place in developmental writing, they can be placed in a course that falls just below college composition or even two courses below college composition. Developmental writing is often multileveled, involving two, sometimes three courses in sequence before college composition, a requirement for many programs, majors, and graduation. Essentially, students who place in developmental writing need the extra assistance in essay organization and development. Beyond the more global issues of academic writing, students may need more of a command of sentence construction, basic grammar, and punctuation.

In essence, there is a range in students who place in developmental writing sequences. On the higher end, there is the student who needs one semester—if that—of support to progress successfully to college composition. On this end, students may need some guidance in strengthening essay organization or development. Or maybe, the student needs practice in responding to texts through writing. The students may even demonstrate some relatively solid command of grammar and punctuation with minor surface areas that can be addressed with some quick lesson reviews and proofing. On the more foundational end of the developmental writing sequences, students may quite realistically struggle with the construction of a simple sentence, let alone the development of a paragraph with a topic sentence and support. Within the sequences of developmental writing and reading, many texts focus upon areas of style, syntax, mechanics, punctuation, and composition that reflect the content addressed in grade school and high school.

In developmental writing, the range between the upper end of the sequence to the more foundational end is quite broad. The students who place into these sequences are just as diverse. On the one hand, you may have students (nontraditional) who simply have been out of school for a number of years. Thus, the developmental writing course provides a structured, hopefully supportive environment to help students refamiliarize themselves with the necessary writing and critical thinking skill sets to progress to composition. Similarly, you may have some more traditional age students (students who just graduated from high school) who just need the extra assistance to strengthen their essay writing—organization and development—with some attention to grammar, punctuation, and mechanics.

However, there are also traditional and nontraditional students who truly struggle with the English language. The struggle is well beyond the comma splice. The struggle rests with the ability to articulate and structure a coherent, syntactically correct simple or compound sentence. Orally, the student may communicate efficiently; however, for these students, the scenario changes with the written sentence literally breaking down. Of course, there is a range of students between both ends of the spectrum. In reality, developmental writing instructors confront a variety of abilities—not that unlike the English instructors of Harvard at the dawn of the twentieth century—from both native English and English as Second Language (ESL) students.

For many developmental students—if not all—you as an instructor are a lifeline because you help students develop their writing skills enough to gain entrance to college composition and the courses that have composition as a corequisite or prerequisite, or any courses that require

31

reports, essay tests, presentational outlines, etc. To add to this role, you are often teaching students who are considered at risk in courses that are considered high risk. Indeed, developmental writing courses are truly important for students, and their purpose in the curricula is manifold.

Approaches to Teaching Developmental Writing

As with all courses, but especially for high-risk ones, careful consideration of your role in the classroom is important. The way you present yourself to your students, the way you interact with your students, how you structure the classroom experience to teach developmental writing— these all reflect some element of your teaching style.

There is quite a bit written on teaching styles; however, to summarize, two basic approaches—with a range between—exist. In sum, instructors may exhibit more teacher-centered or more learner-centered approaches. In turn, these approaches elicit a learning response—passive or active—from students.

Teacher-Centered Teaching

In this style of teaching, the instructor is the sole disseminator of information. Primarily lectured-based classes reflect this style of teaching. To help students learn the content, lecturers need to set a manageable pace for students to follow. Organizing the lecture with a clearly defined introduction, body, and conclusion would help students take more coherent notes. Included within the organization would be transitional words and phrases to help students follow point by point, explanation by explanation, summary by summary, example by example. Even repeating key words and phrases will help reinforce important concepts. In addition, using visuals, writing on boards or overheads, encouraging the students to look at appropriate sections of a text that would reinforce your lecture—all these strategies would help students manage the level of note taking. According to Wilbert J. McKeachie in *Teaching Tips: Strategies, Research, and Theory for College and University Teachers*, effective lectures provide students with the latest information about a subject and can help students make sense of complex material (McKeachie 53). Effective lectures have their benefits, and students do need to learn how to adapt to a lecture format as they progress semester to semester. McKeachie even notes that the lecture, with its long historical roots, is the most common format of teaching in the world

32

(McKeachie 52).   Indeed, lectures with a dynamic, enthusiastic instructor can be quite captivating.

However, strictly lecture-based classes for students placing at the developmental level pose challenges for both the instructor and the student. For the instructor, a strictly lecture-based course can be quite demanding with the level of preparation and the length of the delivery process over time.

For students, especially at the beginning of their college journeys, the strictly lecture format can be overwhelming. According to D. Bok in *Our Underachieving Colleges: A Candid Look at How Students Learn and Why They should be Learning More*, students may only retain about 20 percent of a lecture one week after attending it (Bok123). Over the course of the following weeks, the percentage of the lecture remembered declines even more. In fact, I have known a few students at the developmental level who have dropped out of a strictly lecture-based course—at least in part—because they were not yet equipped for the challenges presented by pace and the amount of note taking, let alone the test taking. Some students who are taking developmental writing may also be attending a college success course—to learn study skills, note-taking strategies, and reading comprehension techniques. The college success courses are often designed to help students learn effective strategies to manage their course work and adjust their learning styles to their instructors' teaching styles, which include lectures. Last, purely lecture-based courses may encourage more passive learning if students are simply taking notes to record rather than engage information.

Learner-Centered Teaching

The opposite of the strictly lecture format teaching style is the learner-centered teaching style. In this style of teaching, the emphasis theoretically centers on the students. In varying degrees, the power within the classroom is shared between student and instructor. According to *Learner-Centered Teaching* by Maryellen Weimer, the goal of this style of teaching "is to equip students with learning skills so sophisticated that they can teach themselves. Power is redistributed in amounts proportional to students' ability to handle it" (Weimer 29). Students may share in the creation of the syllabus, the teaching of the class, even in some of the decision making. However, Weimer does clarify that there are ethical ramifications to this shift in power if not carefully monitored and checked. The instructor has to fulfill his or her responsibilities and ensure that the course is meeting the objectives for the students. For example, in a more learner-centered environment, students, according to Weimer, could be given an opportunity to offer a recommendation, maybe about an assignment: The students are not handed complete oversight (Weimer 31). Weimer does emphasize that there are challenges to this style, particularly for students who are in introductory courses. In essence, the instructor assumes the role of guide and facilitator (Weimer 74).

Active and Passive Learning

Teacher- and learner-centered instruction garners a response from students: Students learn more passively or actively. In sum, active learning encourages students to participate in their own learning rather than assume a solely passive role in a purely lecture-based format (Boylan 101). With regard to learner-centered styles, instructors promote more active learning when they interact with their students, encourage students to interact with the course material, and provide opportunities for their students to interact with and learn from each other. In *What Works: Research-Based Practices in Developmental Education*, Hunter Boylan, a leader in developmental education, reviews much of the research on active and passive learning with regard to developmental education. What Boylan notes is quite interesting. For students who place in developmental education courses (e.g., writing, reading, math), active learning is considered a "best practice" in teaching predominately because more traditional learning environments, which favor lecture and drill and practice approaches, did not work for these students when they were in high school. Active learning encourages higher order thinking; it calls for students to explore the knowledge firsthand. Even more beneficially, active learning, particularly for low achieving students, helps improve writing and reading (Boylan 101-102). In essence, active learning itself engages traditional students, nontraditional students, and the at-risk students.

Active learning strategies assume many forms. In *Teaching Tips,* Wilbert J. McKeachie notes that active learning primarily centers on discussion (McKeachie 30). However, whether the discussion is in large group, small groups, or pairs, discussion is not the only way students learn actively. Problem-solving activities certainly can be linked with process writing and grammar. For example, students can strengthen their editing and proofing skills by analyzing a paragraph or essay that needs improvement with the thesis or organization. In developmental writing courses that are grammar intensive, students can analyze a sentence or paragraph with grammar errors. Independently or even paired, students can identify the error through analysis and propose possible solutions, even evaluating which solution would be the most effective. Journal writing can be included to help students think about how they might apply a particular class lesson to an essay assignment or how the lesson might be applied to essays in other classes. Students can be asked to reflect on a particular reading and its relevance personally and academically. Students can use their journals to initiate the essay writing process through brainstorming or free writing about a particular topic. Students could even use their journal to reflect on how they go about learning and writing their essays, a more metacognitive approach. The developmental writing classroom appears to be an excellent base to support active learning. However, this base does not dismiss some effective elements of the lecture style. Well-organized, brief lectures can be used to set up class lessons, to review course material, to make connections between assignments, and to interject relevant, real-life examples of practical application. The brief mini lessons can be sprinkled with questions posed to students. In *How College Affects Students*, Ernest T. Pascarella and Patrick T. Terenzini conclude that flexibility and varied instructional styles linked with active learning may encourage student development: intellectual competence in subject matter; emotion management; mature interpersonal relationships; identity formation; purpose formation; and integrity development (23). In the end, you as an instructor need to be flexible enough to discover what works effectively for you and your students.

The Reading-Writing Connections in a Developmental Writing-Specific Course

When you teach a developmental writing course, it is important to remember the connection with reading. With regard to course structures, developmental writing and reading come in several forms. Many colleges offer specific leveled courses for developmental writing and reading—treating the subjects separately for a more in-depth focus. Still, other colleges combine developmental writing and reading courses to recognize more formally the interconnections. In some cases, the actual credit structure for a combined writing and reading course may be four credits or even six credits. Regardless of the actual structure, it is important to remember the interconnections between reading and writing.

According to Mina Shaughnessy in "Some New Approaches toward Teaching," writing involves creative reading. Shaughnessy explains that quite literally writing "is the encoding of speech into lines of print or script that are in turn decoded into speech by a reader," leading to the connections among speech, writing, and reading (Shaughnessy 3). While these interconnections may be reflective in many types of, if not all, writing, they are particularly noteworthy with process writing (taking students through various stages from prewriting to revision). The prewriting activities (e.g., topic generation, brainstorming, free writing, and even clustering or mapping) involve the creative mind, encouraging students to explore their topics for essay writing both concretely and abstractly. However, the creative side to writing and reading is inevitably linked with the critical thinking side, where students read the pages of their brainstorming or free writing. They read with the intent to make sense of their thoughts, to see connections among the ideas, to summarize, and to analyze what they have generated. When they move from the prewriting to drafting stages of writing an essay, students use their critical thinking skills to organize their ideas, develop their ideas, synthesize their ideas, and even evaluate their ideas. In process writing, students are continually reading and ultimately evaluating their ideas. Some students may be encouraged by their instructors to read their writing aloud to themselves and maybe even others. Especially with the role of computers, students can write, read, and revise. In other words, students need their reading skills to make sense of their writing as they move from the prewriting to revision. In essence, students engage their critical thinking.

While the writing process is intricately linked with the reading processes of students, students may also write in response to fiction and nonfiction, more literary and more technical types of writing. Depending on the level of developmental writing, students may be introduced to very basic response to readings. Some instructors may start the process by teaching students how to summarize a selection and then move from summary into more reflective types of writing in response to the reading. Asking students to determine whether or not they can make personal connections with the readings is a way for them to interact with the selection. Of course, bringing the reading into the context of large group or small group discussions simply provides many opportunities for idea generation, reflection, and analysis of passages, which all can be connected to the writing process.

However, some developmental writing courses, just below composition, at times will take the integration of readings a few steps farther. On this level, some developmental writing courses will build on the summarization and reflection by teaching students how to analyze (identify topic, main points, and support), and evaluate (have students offer their judgment on the reading selection's value) different reading selections. Other developmental writing sequences may be structured to teach students how to work with and integrate sources into their essays through paraphrases and quotations—the basic MLA format for in-text citations and Works Cited. Again, though, the focus of each developmental writing course does vary from college to college with regard to the extent that reading is integrated. In essence, the writing course is an ideal place to show students the interconnections between their reading and writing.

Structuring or Framing the Class Lesson

Lesson Planning

Before you as an instructor even enter the classroom the first day, so much thought goes into teaching developmental writing. It's not unusual for instructors of developmental education, or with any course, to be patient and understanding with their students. However, it is just as important for instructors to be patient and understanding with themselves as they structure their class lessons. In addition to patience and understanding, instructors need to be flexible. At times, as an instructor, you may need to revisit the course schedule or calendar portion of your syllabus to allow more time or reduce time allotted to a class activity. You may even find that you planned for more than can be reasonably accomplished in the semester. Even outside forces, such as inclement weather or power outages, may impact your need for flexibility. Indeed, each instructor approaches lesson planning differently; some even build flextime into their syllabi.

Not withstanding the adjustments in pace and scheduling, there are some basic elements to consider when planning the lesson for a particular class period or week. Organize your lesson around an introduction, a body, and a conclusion. Even if you implement more learner-centered teaching, the structure of the lesson still has a beginning, a middle, and an end. With the learner-centered format, you need to be open enough to allow time for the discussion and the activities to flourish, but also mindful enough to initiate closure and/or progression to ensure that you have met what you and your students have set out to accomplish.

Activities to Begin Class

Generally, each instructor has a particular style and favors certain practical and/or creative strategies for opening a class. Sharing ideas with colleagues or attending teaching-related workshops help to generate a pool of techniques from which you can always draw. Even keeping a folder or teaching log can be helpful for recording ideas for future use. As an instructor, you need to make the decision on what works best for your students. While each class period may be designed to flow seamlessly from the period before and into the next one, each class session, though, does start anew.

Welcome and Announcements

For beginning a class, one surefire technique that transitions students into class time is your "welcome back to class," which may include relevant announcements of campus activities or even acknowledgements of student success.

Attendance

The taking of attendance may also help signal the start of class for students. Attendance policies vary from instructor to instructor. Some instructors may use the beginning of class to note the presence of their students. However, there are others who may wait a bit for an opportunity to take attendance when the students are engaged in an activity, and still some other instructors may prefer to mark attendance toward the conclusion of class. Attendance could be formally taken by an instructor, or, in other cases, instructors may use a sign-in sheet. There are cases when absenteeism may be challenging to address. To deal with this issue, instructors tap into their creativity. As a means of encouraging regular attendance, some instructors may use the beginning of class for a brief reflective or journal activity with points attached. In other cases, some instructors assign a brief quiz on a homework assignment. Views on attendance differ, and the ways instructors observe or document attendance varies just as much. In some colleges, instructors may be required by contract to keep accurate student attendance records.

The Syllabus and the Lesson's Objectives

Reviewing the lesson's objectives or relevant parts of the syllabus outline also signals the start of class. For example, request that your students take out the calendar portion of their syllabi. You or one of your students can read the section that is relevant for the class period. This provides an opportunity for you and your students to look ahead for due dates to essay assignments and make connections among the many lessons. If you model for your students how to review a syllabus outline, hopefully your students will develop the habit of regularly reviewing their syllabi to manage their schedules and homework assignments.

In addition to a brief syllabus review, you may briefly point out the objectives of the class lessons, so students have some sense of direction. When discussing the objectives, you can make any relevant connections to homework or essay assignments. Of course, at the end of class, there is an opportunity to review homework assignments and due dates, as well.

Gauging Student Knowledge

Once the recordkeeping is completed, the beginning of class can be utilized to gauge the students' knowledge about the class lesson. This technique can work in two ways. First, you can ask students to summarize the key points learned from the previous class lesson. As an instructor, this gives you an opportunity to gauge the recall of your students. It also gives you an opportunity to determine if any additional review of the previous class lesson is needed. Second, you can ask your students if they know anything about the lesson of focus for the class period. For example, if the lesson revolves around the basic paragraph structure or how to develop a paragraph with evidence, ask your students some questions about paragraph structure or evidence: Does anyone know what a paragraph does, or what parts make up a paragraph? What is evidence? What types of evidence do writers use to support points? The purpose is to gain a broader perspective of what knowledge your students' possess and then build on that knowledge to accomplish your objective. Once you engage in the dialogue with your students, create a transition or bridge that connects your questions with the lesson or activities.

Posing questions and engaging in dialogue are productive ways to interact with your students: They are sharpening their listening skills, their critical thinking skills, and their oral communication skills. However, what if you have a particularly quiet, shy group? Or what if you have a group with only a few who speak or even monopolize the discussion? There are some techniques to engage the entire class. Instead of putting students on the spot to respond to some opening questions, have your students write their responses to your question on an index card or a piece of notebook paper. After posing the question, give your students some time to reflect and jot down their responses. Then, provide each student an opportunity to share his or her response. Basically, this strategy affords every student an opportunity to share his or her thoughts at least once. This strategy also acts as an ice breaker and can potentially generate some interesting discussion.

Having students jot down their thoughts on index cards or notebook paper can be quite handy, but there are some variations that can be utilized as well. If you use the index cards and you would like to jazz things up, use index cards in a variety of colors. Poster-size paper can also be used. Students can record their responses and then stick or tape the poster-size paper on the

39

wall. If there are no funds for the index cards or poster-size paper, have students (a few at a time), scribe their abbreviated responses on the chalkboard or equivalent. Then, with the board filled with comments, have the students go around and share their thoughts. As the instructor, you can give each student an opportunity to speak before taking the lesson to the next step, or you can engage your students in additional discussion.

Giving your students an opportunity to articulate their thoughts in writing extends to more reflective pieces as well. Perhaps the chapter of your text begins with an interesting quotation or a picture. You certainly can have your students reflect in their journals or notebooks on the quotation or the picture, eventually helping your students draw links between the picture or quotation and the lesson. As with the index cards, you can have your students share some lines from their journals. Index cards, journals, notebook paper—all become vehicles for your students to record their thoughts and share them aloud. Again, these techniques permit every student in class the opportunity to participate on some level. Indeed, many of the activities to begin a class can be used throughout class, as well.

Activities to Sustain Class

To create some variety, collaborative learning can also be incorporated into a class session. *Collaborative*, *cooperative*, and *peer learning* are terms used to describe bringing students together in pairs or larger groups to learn and work with each other (Maxwell 163). Collaborative, cooperative, and peer learning have their own nuances, but for the purpose of this discussion, the term collaborative will be used. For those who favor more learner-centered teaching styles, group work of some form can be an enriching way to provide students the time to problem solve through collaboration. Historically, the use of groups as a means of learning predates pre-Revolutionary America. In fact, Benjamin Franklin advocated this type of learning outside university settings as a means of advancing an individual's knowledge in a time when access to university-based education was limited (Maxwell 164). Today as then, the use of collaboration has value.

Depending on the activity, groups can be formed in a variety of sizes. Groups can range from approximately three to six students, so it is important that students be given a few moments to assemble into their groups. If there is limited space within the classroom to arrange students comfortably in groups, you can simply join students who are seated closest to each other. On the other hand, with some planning, you could also carefully consider the students for each group. As the semester progresses, you will have a better understanding of the student dynamics within your class, and you can plan accordingly. However, it is important to consider time, set up, and manageability.

When you first introduce group work into your class, you need to invest a few extra minutes to acclimate the class to the collaboration.

- Establish the objectives of the lesson and explain how the collaboration will help achieve the lesson.

- Provide step-by-step directions for the class and the individual groups. Even writing some abbreviated directions on the board or in a handout can assist students in their groups.

- Identify roles for the students within the groups. For students who are new to group work, consider assigning or having the students within the group identify roles. Based on the goal of the lesson, the roles of each group member may vary. While all members of the group are responsible for discussing the assignment, there are a few basic tasks that can be assigned to group members. All students could be taking notes, but at least have one or two with the task of **note taker or scribe**. In addition to the note taker, identify the group **facilitator**, the person who will try to keep the discussion on track. Last, there are additional roles that can be assigned to all or just one or two. **Researchers** can locate information in their texts. Though all group members may share information aloud, the **spokesperson** can be the person who, on behalf of the group, articulates the group's findings to the entire class.

- Visit each group. Especially for students new to group work, visit each group to review the directions and to ensure that group members understand their roles. This visit also allows you to gauge the group's progress on the assignment.

- Discuss. Once the groups have been given the allotted time to work on their assignments, bring the class back to your attention. Have each group report its findings to the entire class. Students can share their findings from their seats, or the groups could also be brought to the front of the room to address the class. If you wanted to utilize an overhead, the group's notes could be projected to the class. In the absence of an overhead or equivalent technology, students could even jot their notes on the board. If the resources are available, you could give (at the beginning of the activity) each group a poster-size piece of paper and a marker, so they can record their notes. From this poster-size paper, groups can showcase their findings to the class.

- Sum up. Once you are done with the group work or the task, summarize what the class has learned from the group reports or even ask for a couple of students to sum up the information learned from all the groups. This space for summary allows you time to offer any additional comments, even linking the closure of the activity to the lesson's objectives.

- Transition to your next class activity.

When carefully planned, group work offers students an opportunity to participate in an exercise that engages their critical thinking and enhances their interpersonal communication. For the instructor, collaborative learning offers some variety in the delivery of the course content.

Group work can be extended to outside the classroom, as well. If you want students to work in groups on a project outside class time, be sure to set up the groups and the assignment with clearly articulated directions. In fact, once the students are assigned their groups, have the students exchange contact information and set up the time and place for their meeting. The students can even meet at the college library or campus center before or after class if their schedules permit.

For commuter students especially, group projects that require outside class time can be quite challenging. For one, students may struggle to identify common meeting times. As the instructor, you could suggest that they keep in touch on the phone or through e-mail. If students have access to a course management system, such as Blackboard or Blackboard WebCT, you could set up some of the group activity online for the students. In order to use a course management system, though, students might need some training. Attendance could be another challenge. On the one hand, group work makes everyone in the group accountable and responsible for contributing. On the other hand, when a student is absent or does not contribute equally, the responsibility shifts to the other members and presents considerable dilemmas when the project comes due. To obtain feedback and insight into the group dynamics, you could have students evaluate the functionality of the group and their roles within the group. Individually, students can write a brief report or respond to questions that you composed on a handout.

In sum, collaboration—in or outside class—teaches students to work with others, as it engages both their creative and critical thinking. It also places some responsibility for learning upon the students themselves. Even more, collaborative learning promotes leadership skills because fully vested group member may demonstrate initiative, responsiveness, and management.

The developmental writing class offers possibilities for collaboration within and outside class time; however, for the collaborative work to have a chance at success, careful planning, manageability, and oversight are needed.

Pairings

If you would like to integrate another type of collaborative work in a class lesson, consider "Think, Pair, Share." This type of paired effort works quite well as an alternative to groups (three or more students). A developmental writing course is certainly intensive with regard to workload for the students and the instructor. Given the workload, you may not be able to spare the time for group work, or sometimes, you may have a class not conducive to group work (students who don't get along or who chat too much). I first learned about the "Think, Pair, Share" technique from a college success text entitled *Keys to Success: Creating Powerful Habits of Mind* by Carol Carter Joyce Bishop, and Sarah Lyman Kravits and have adopted into my developmental writing class. As with larger groups, you need to set up the activity, identify the pairs, and provide the objective:

- Provide clearly defined directions for the pairs to follow.
- Give students an index card or have them take out a sheet of paper to jot down notes.
- Have each student individually respond to or think about the task within a certain time allotment.
- Join the pairs, so they can share their responses to the task with each other. To help guide the discussion between the pairs, offer some areas of focus. For example, the paired students can note the similarities and differences in their responses to the task.
- Have the pairs share their insights to the entire class.

This activity provides a very productive segue into class discussion and affords each student, including a reluctant or shy one, an opportunity to contribute. When you are ready to close this activity and transition to the next segment of class, offer some final thoughts linking the activity to the lesson's objective.

Independent Activities

To create some balance with the group work, you can also allocate some class time for more independent work. Reflecting in journals, writing sample introductions, editing paragraphs for consistency in point of view, responding to questions—there are many developmental writing activities that engage students more independently to help reinforce the lessons.

Your Assignment

To create more engaging lessons, think about some activities that may be integrated coherently into a class period. To focus on work particularly relevant to a developmental writing class, consider the following list of action verbs: reflect, write, edit, proof, practice, discuss, and collaborate. What in-class activities might you create or integrate from your text that would have your students demonstrating these elements to varying degrees throughout the semester?

Reflect:_____

Write:_____

Edit:_____

Proof:_____

Practice:_____

Discuss:_____

Collaborate:_____

Certainly, you may think of additional ways to create an environment that fosters learning, but a place to start would be with any one of the seven action verbs.

When planning a class lesson, think about how you as an instructor want students to learn, understand, and demonstrate the course content. Varying the strategies used to deliver the lesson keeps the class interested and tends to appeal to different learners. Regardless of the strategies, keep the lessons organized, unified, and coherent. Show progression among the different class lessons, so students understand the connections among writing, reading, and discussing.

Activities to Conclude a Class

Some of the same practical, creative activities used to begin class can also be used to conclude class. However, there are a few additional techniques to consider.

The One-Minute Paper

As a pedagogical technique, the one-minute paper generally takes place at the end of class. To gauge the level of learning or lesson comprehension, the instructor asks students one question (Pascarella 113). The question, of course, would be tailored to your lesson and your purpose—what you hope to glean from the students' responses. For a developmental writing class, there are many options for questions: What important information did you learn today that you can use in your next essay assignment? Of the different introductory strategies reviewed today, which one might you use to begin your next essay? What do you think was the main point learned from today's reading assignment? Do you agree or disagree with the author's main points from today's reading assignment? In practice, though, the one-minute paper may be transformed into the two minute- or the three-minute paper. How you choose to use this instructional technique is certainly your decision. For students, this technique provides an opportunity to reflect upon or sum up the day's lessons. For instructors, this technique provides some insight into what students comprehended or failed to comprehend. In sum, this technique allows you to be proactive. If you discovered that you need to re-address a lesson or clarify a point, you can plan the next class lesson accordingly. If appropriate, you can even ask students to share their responses from the one-minute paper to the class.

Summary of Key Lessons

To close a class, you can briefly summarize the lesson's objectives and review the way that they were accomplished. If you do not want to assume this task, ask for student volunteers to summarize the lesson or link the lesson to the objectives.

Reminders

Before they exit or as they pack to leave, you can remind your students of any homework assignments, special directions, or even the area of focus for the next class period, so students can understand the interconnections between one class period and the next.

Helping Students Sustain Good Writing Practices Outside Class

More and more, students use e-mail to communicate with their instructors outside class time. In fact, there are instructors who prefer that students submit electronic versions of their writings through e-mail or a course management system. This out-of-class communication offers a wonderful opportunity for students to apply and practice their newfound writing knowledge. Even if the e-mail is meant to be relatively short, students can still practice coherent paragraph organization and appropriate grammar, punctuation, and spelling. In an age of text messaging, a mini lesson in e-mail etiquette will help students realize that the first-person pronoun "I" is actually capitalized, and the second-person pronoun "you" is actually three letters, not the lower case "u." If you use e-mail quite a bit with your students, you certainly have the option to establish e-mail etiquette to your specifications, including how your students identify themselves or their course section in the subject line of the e-mail. Thus, a mini lesson on e-mail composition shows students how their knowledge of paragraphing, grammar, punctuation, and spelling will help them in technical writing or writing for other purposes and audiences.

Integrating College Success Skills into Developmental English

Considering instructional styles, structuring class lessons, even establishing e-mail etiquette—indeed, teaching developmental writing encompasses much. There is, though, even more to bear in mind. The developmental writing classroom fosters a wonderful opportunity to reinforce college success skills.

Within the last 30 years, with the advent of the student success movement, more and more emphasis has been placed on teaching students skills to help them study, take tests, set goals, and manage their schedules. However, the need for some type of student success skills instruction is not new. By 1909, more than 350 colleges in the United States offered some form of study skills course, which included some focus on improving reading comprehension. With the increase of courses came the necessity for a course-specific text, and by 1920 colleges and universities had approximately 100 books from which to select (Casazza 20).

The texts themselves ranged from a focus on the development of a single skill to the development of a series of related skills. At the turn of the twentieth century, if students needed instruction on study skills, *How to Study: Hints to Students in College and High Schools* by John Schulte had long been available, as it was published in 1877. On another front, *Methods of Mind-*

Training; Concentrated Attention and Memory (1896) by Catherine Aiken could prove useful for students requiring stronger focus. Even into the twentieth century, the need for study skills texts flourished. Students could scrutinize *How to Study Effectively; A Guide to Students in Developing and Improving Habits of Studying and Learning* (1938) by Frank Par. To keep up with their instructors' lectures, students could prepare with *Note-Taking* (1910) by Samuel Swayze Seward, Jr.; *Suggestions for Note Taking* (1910) by Ezra Kempton Maxfield; or even *Outlining as a Study Procedure* (1930) by William Alexander Barton, Jr. A more comprehensive text called *Making the Most of One's Mind* (1915) by John Adams not only schooled students in note taking and study but also listening, examinations, textbooks, reading, and even essay writing. To learn study strategies coupled with time management, students could peruse William F. Book's *Learning How to Study and Work Effectively; A Contribution to the Psychology of Personal Efficiency* (1926). In fact, as the twentieth century progressed, college students were being studied so that other college students could learn good habits. The results of one such report served as the basis for *Student's Guide to Efficient Study; A Manual Based on the Results of Scientific Investigations into the Study Habits of College Students* (1931) by Luelia Pressey and Jessie Mary Ferguson. Essentially, the teaching of student success skills still persists.

Today, over 90 percent of two-year colleges, according to the *Second National Survey of First-Year Academic Practices*, offer some type of first-year seminar or student success course (John N. Gardner Institute for Excellence in Undergraduate Education-formerly known as the Policy Center on the First Year of College 14). The goals of these courses, though, are not limited to study skills, goal setting, note taking, and time management. Learning style assessment and career exploration play a significant role in college success or freshman seminar courses. However, research suggests that these "personal management skills" traditionally taught in freshman seminar or college success courses need to be integrated as well into developmental courses, such as writing and reading. In "Establishing Personal Management Training in Developmental Education and First-Year Curricula," Robert Nelson argues, "To enable students to gain of their academic agendas, personal management training must be integrated with the developmental and first-year curricula….Students must have the opportunity to observe, recognize, develop, and exercise goal-setting principles, project-planning techniques, time management habits, and stress management strategies" (Nelson 171). Most certainly, developmental writing courses are intensive for the students and the instructors. How, then, can a

47

developmental writing course also include personal management training when the focus on achieving the writing outcomes is time consuming enough?

Some students who are taking a developmental writing course might be taking a college success or freshman seminar course, as well. For these students, the terms *goal setting, planning,* and *time management* will sound familiar. However, for students who are not participating in a college success course, the terms may be relatively new with regard to course work. Regardless of the possibilities, there are ways to integrate goal setting, project planning, and time management into developmental writing classes. First, use the syllabus or course schedule as a vehicle to discuss goals and planning times. Get students into the habit of looking at their course schedules at the beginning of class or at a convenient time—even at the end of class.

What is the purpose of this? With your helpful explanations, you can point out the lessons that will be covered in a given week and any due dates for assignments linked with those lessons. Ultimately, you can help your students see the relationships between setting a goal (e.g., to complete and hand in an essay assignment) and actually achieving the goal. In order to hand in their essay assignment on time, students need to plan not only with their writing course in mind but also with their other commitments in mind. One week may appear to be plenty of time to compose a five-paragraph essay; however, for students who have to balance their other courses and possibly a work schedule, the hours available to complete the assignment shrink dramatically. Consider reminding students that they have to do some planning in order to complete and hand in their essays. They need to examine their current schedules for the week; prioritize the assignments that need to get done first; and then set enough time aside in order to write their essays. You can even ask your students to plot out their schedule for completing their assignment in a planner or on a calendar. Including these brief reminders can help students understand the connections between handing in an assignment and advanced planning.

The college success strategies go beyond goal setting and time management. The skills and strategies include studying and note taking. If you want your students to take notes on a particular lesson, remind your students, at least at the beginning of the term, to write down the material that you place on the board. Remind students that this material is important to a particular assignment. Of course, there will be students who automatically come to class prepared to take plenty of notes; however, there will also be students who are not familiar with effective note taking and who will not make a connection between the information that you place on the board and an assignment. Some students, most certainly, need to be reminded to bring a notebook to class and to open their notebooks at the beginning of class, so they can take notes. College success and freshman seminar courses often contain lessons on different note-taking strategies, but it would be even more reinforcing if you can use clear transitions, explanations, and examples to help keep students organized in their thoughts as they are writing their notes in class. To get your students more actively involved, you can ask them to summarize in their own words the information that you reviewed or wrote on the board. To gauge if your students understand some elements of a lesson, you can even assign a one-minute paper at the end of class. Or in the beginning of the next class, ask students to summarize the lesson learned in the previous class.

In addition to the note-taking, goal-setting, and time management reminders, you may need to reinforce some study strategies. In fact, in *Yes We Can! A Community College Guide for Developing American's Underprepared*, author Robert H. McCabe suggests that "instructors can improve students' understanding of study by modeling the desired behavior or skill" (91). Think of the study skills modeling in much of the same way that you can model effective time management, goal setting, and note taking skills for students. If you are reviewing a chapter from the text, you can point out, or have your students point out, some of the important information that is needed for study or in the writing of their papers. Be attentive to the chapter title, the chapter objectives, the headings and subheadings, key words in bold or italics, charts, sample paragraphs or essays, and end-of-the-chapter summaries. In essence, you or your students can model the SQ3R method or a modified version of it appropriate for class.

SQ3R is a study method often taught to students in reading and study skills courses. With this method, students prepare to read a text chapter by **surveying** the outline of the chapter; **questioning** how the material is related to class or the assignment; **reading** the chapter through; **reciting** key information or summaries to reinforce their comprehension; and **reviewing** their notes or relevant sections to help reinforce their comprehension. When you review the material from a text with students, you can even remind them of especially important information (e.g., a page with a model essay or list of transitional words or phrases) that they need to review before they study for a quiz or compose an essay. If you want to involve your students more actively, ask for a volunteer to identify important pages needed to be reviewed before students sit down to compose their essays or study for a quiz. If you want students to read a chapter from the text actively, remind them to keep a pen or pencil in hand to underline key points or to note questions that they may need to ask in class. These reinforcements, at least at the beginning of the semester, help students form effective habits as the semester progresses.

Given the intensity of just getting students to meet the course outcomes by the end of the term, you may believe that reinforcing—albeit briefly—success skills or habits falls outside your purview as an instructor and certainly outside the scope of the course. Indeed, developmental writing is not a study skills course in the way that a freshman seminar or college success course functions, nor do you have the time to address study skills comprehensively. However, writing and reading go hand in hand as do the skills that support writing and reading effectively. Think of goal setting, time management planning, effective study techniques, and other relevant skills as the support necessary for students to master the academic course content of developmental writing. The key is to locate small pockets of opportunities to reinforce the skills.

Before you enter the classroom on the first day, think carefully about your own teaching style, the structure of the lesson, and the support skills necessary for your students to master the academic content. Remember the statistics from chapter 1: Over a million students each year enroll in at least one remedial course with approximately 25 percent of students dropping out (McCabe 45). Much of the literature about first-year students, particularly those needing developmental courses, insist that within the first six months of college life, students will decide whether or not to return. Nearly half of first-year students make the decision not to return for the second year (McCabe 60). While these are national statistics, your college, through the institutional research office, may track its own numbers. Despite the best of efforts, there may be a myriad of personal reasons for student attrition that go beyond your control as an instructor and beyond what your college can address.

Developmental writing courses are often taken—though not always—within the first semester or two of a student's college experience. Ultimately, an important course, such as developmental writing, is taken during a pivotal transition period for students, and you, as an instructor, are on the front lines of this experience.

Helpful Hints

- Consider practical and creative ways to open and close each class session.

- Try to remember your students' names. Engage your students in brief conversation, if possible, before and/or after class. The connection makes a difference.

- Think about varying class activities to reach course objectives and engage students. If you are uncertain about how to add some interest to a lesson on a particular day, consider what you could include that would have students demonstrate reflecting, writing, editing, proofing, practicing, collaborating, or discussing. Also, integrate independent, paired, and group activities when and where appropriate.

- Bear in mind the need to reinforce some basic college success skills to help students prepare, plan, finish, and submit their assignments.

CHAPTER 4

Appealing to Different Learners in Class Activities

Objectives:

- *To raise awareness of learning styles*

- *To create classroom activities that reach different learners*

- *To move beyond the lecture*

From the moment that you accept your developmental writing assignment to the moment you meet your class for the first time, you have been quite involved with reviewing your text, learning about the support services, creating a syllabus for your course, and even contemplating the structure of your lesson format. Indeed, all your preparation for class reflects your style as an instructor. However, once you enter the classroom, you will discover whether or not your teaching style connects—or maybe even collides—with the varied student learning styles.

Today, learning style theories serve as the very foundation of many developmental writing texts. Yet the connection between writing courses and learning is not new. In fact, the connection between the teaching of writing and the learning of writing locates itself in earlier texts. In the text *Freshman Composition* (1897), Henry G. Pearson, instructor in English at the Massachusetts Institute of Technology, divides his text into four key sections—the composition, the paragraph, the sentence, and the words. Yesterday and today, these very sections still occupy a significant place in the multiple levels of developmental writing texts. In 1897, though, Pearson set his *Freshman Composition* apart from other college writing textbooks because he dubbed his text an "experiment." In the Introduction to Pearson's *Freshman Composition*, Professor Arlo Bates explains:

A student learns to write as a boy learns to swim,—by doing it. In these days nobody would attempt to teach composition by mere theorizing, any more than one would attempt to teach swimming on dry land. In actual practice the learner does not write first words, then sentences, then paragraphs, and defer the attempt to produce a complete theme until he has mastered these. (Pearson ix)

Notwithstanding the gender bias with regard to the textbook audience, Bates raises a compelling point about the student's learning process. Essentially, Bates acknowledges the importance of "bodily-kinesthetic" learning, a type of learning that actively involves students by "doing." In this case, students in this MIT class will be writing rather than solely listening to lectures on composition theory. Even more, the responsibility, as the Introduction articulates, for teaching composition does not rest solely upon the instructor. The students share some responsibility in the education process, as well:

The success of any teacher of course depends less upon the text-book than upon the personal equation. The ideal text-book is a volume which furnishes necessary facts and the best system of mastering and arranging them, but which leaves to the teacher the part of presenting them and to the pupil the task of grasping and assimilating. No teacher makes a student master the difficult art of composition. He can at most but direct and assist, so that the efforts of the learner shall be exercised to the best advantage. (Quoted in Pearson x–xi)

At the close of the nineteenth century, a composition text designed for freshmen at MIT acknowledges essentially the need to incorporate more learner-centered, kinesthetic activity in the teaching of writing. Today, the need for students to be more actively involved in the learning of writing persists, as does the need for students and instructors to recognize the variety of ways that learning is processed.

Learning Styles

In brief, learning styles are the different ways students gain knowledge, process, remember, and apply course material (Pascarella 139). More and more, course textbooks or technological support materials in developmental English include learning style self-diagnostic questionnaires or surveys for students to partake. Essentially, students are asked to respond to a question or statement by checking whether or not it reflects a personal preference or by ranking (e.g., most-to-least like me). Once they tabulate the results, students discover their learning preferences—the most efficient ways that they process information. For example, some students may be more bodily-kinesthetic in that they comprehend material by being more actively involved in the learning; others may be more auditory in that they prefer listening to explanations of material; still others may be more visual in that they can learn best from images, graphs, diagrams— seeing. Even more, students can learn from all three basic methods. There are, though, different types of surveys and instruments that can be used to interpret learning styles beyond the basic auditory, visual, and kinesthetic learners.

In *How College Affects Students*, Pascarella and Terenzini conclude from the research on learning styles that students "demonstrate significantly higher levels of knowledge acquisition when they are exposed to instruction that matches their preferred learning style than when they are exposed to instruction that does not" (139). In other words, a student understands the course material better from an instructor who appeals to his or her preferred way of learning. For example, a student who learns best by seeing would learn the material better from an instructor who communicates the lesson with effective visuals. This scenario, though, does not truly reflect the reality of the classroom experience for all students and instructors who have their own styles of teaching.

One benefit for students to understand their learning styles is that they not only understand their strengths but also their challenges. What happens when students are faced with a learning environment that does not foster their preferred method of learning for various instructor or subject-related reasons? Once students understand their strengths, they can also learn techniques and strategies to help them process and learn course material outside their comfort zone. For example, if a student learns best through seeing but has an instructor who favors more verbal-linguistic methods in teaching the course, perhaps the student could transpose some lecture notes into graphs, charts, or other visuals to help comprehend the material more effectively. Oftentimes, the domain of learning styles as linked with note taking and study skills falls within the purview of college success or reading courses. However, today, effective learning strategy reviews are reaching developmental writing texts, as well.

Through instruction manuals or annotated instructor textbooks, more and more developmental-level writing books offer learning style inventories for students, as well as suggestions and activities that instructors can adopt to reach a variety of different learners within the classroom. In fact, some of the technological support that accompanies some developmental English texts, such as MyWritingLab and MyReadingLab, offer online learning style assessments. If your students are taking a college success or freshman seminar, they probably have taken a learning styles inventory. As an instructor, if you are interested in taking a survey to identify your own learning and teaching preferences, there are online sites that offer learning style inventories. Even more, some colleges offer online learning style assessment on their Web sites or in their career or learning centers.

There are a variety of assessments that you may come across. The Kolb Learning Style Inventory is one such assessment. The inventory grounds itself in more experiential learning theories and ultimately categorizes students' approaches to learning (Kolb 8). The four categories include: concrete experience, reflective observations, abstract conceptualization, and active experimentation. Essentially, students may learn whether or not they prefer the concrete or the abstract and action or reflection (Kolb 12). The ultimate aim is to increase students' metacognition, awareness of the process by which they learn, so they can monitor and ultimately better manage their learning (Kolb 8). More information about this inventory can be located at www.learningfromexperience.com.

Another type of learning styles inventory that you may encounter is the VARK (**v**isual, **a**ural, **r**ead/write, **k**inesthetic) Guide to Learning Styles. Basically, the VARK will help students understand the process by which they take in information, so they can study and take tests more effectively by exploring the visual (V), aural (A), read/write (R), kinesthetic (K), multimodal (MM) strategies for study. More information can be located at www.vark-learn.com.

Essentially, the Kolb Learning Styles Inventory and The VARK Guide to Learning Styles are only two. Just as there are assessments that give insight into the learning process, there are assessments that give insight into students' personalities or dispositions—all in an attempt to allow students to interact with their environment with more understanding and awareness. In fact, The Myers-Briggs Personality Type Indicator and the Keirsey Temperament Sorter (www.keirsey.com) have been modified and integrated into different college success texts, particularly the *Keys to Success* Series by Carol Carter, Joyce Bishop, and Sara Kravits. Not unusually, learning style and personality type indicators are integrated into more skills-based college success and developmental reading texts. The ultimate goal of many of these assessments is to encourage students to think metacognitively: to think about themselves and how they interact with others and their world; to think about how they learn and how they might strengthen their learning.

How, then, does knowing about your students' learning styles ultimately shape your teaching pedagogy? From chapter 3, recall the reference to the developmental education researcher Hunter Boylan. In *What Works: Research-Based Practices in Developmental Education*, Boylan concludes that for students who place in developmental education courses (e.g., writing, reading, math), active learning is considered a "best practice." The more traditional learning environments, which favor lecture and drill-and-practice approaches, failed students when they were in high school. Thus, active learning, particularly for low-achieving students, helps improve writing and reading (Boylan 101–102).

Even if your course does not provide a formal learning styles inventory, as an instructor, you can still offer lessons that tap into different learning styles. Diverse, creative approaches to instruction would help integrate more active learning into a classroom. At the very least, considering ways to hone instruction may help you evaluate your teaching methods—what is or is not working effectively—as you assist your students in meeting course outcomes by the semester's end.

The multiple intelligences approach to learning style preference, for instance, affords a manageable way to think about teaching and learning with or without knowing your students' specific styles.

Multiple Intelligences

To vary the delivery of your class lessons and to engage different student learning styles, consider the insight gleaned from Howard Gardner's multiple intelligences. In 1983, Harvard University professor Howard Gardner published *Frames of Mind: Theory of Multiple Intelligences*, which challenges the more traditional view of intelligence or IQ by arguing that individuals possess a variety of different intelligences, some intelligences being more prominent than others. In sum, multiple intelligences or preferences include the following: (1) verbal-linguistic, (2) logical-mathematical, (3) bodily-kinesthetic, (4) visual-spatial, (5) intrapersonal, (6) interpersonal, (7) musical, and (8) naturalistic.

In *Keys to Effective Learning: Developing Powerful Habits of Mind*, authors Carol Carter, Joyce Bishop, and Sarah Lyman Kravits provide a user-friendly list describing each intelligence in terms of a student's abilities:

Verbal-Linguistic

- Ability to communicate through language (listening, reading, writing, speaking)

Logical-Mathematical

- Ability to understand logical reasoning and problem solving (math, science, patterns, sequences)

Bodily-Kinesthetic

- Ability to use physical body skillfully and to take in knowledge through bodily sensation (coordination, working with hands)

Visual-Spatial

- Ability to understand spatial relationships and to perceive and create images (visual art, graphic design, charts and maps)

Interpersonal

- Ability to relate to others, noticing their moods, motivations, and feelings (social activity, cooperative learning, teamwork)

Intrapersonal

- Ability to understand one's own behavior and feelings (self-awareness, independence, time spent alone)

Musical

- Ability to comprehend and create meaningful sound and recognize patterns (music, sensitivity to sound and patterns)

Naturalistic

- Ability to understand features of the environment (interests in nature, environmental balance, ecosystem, stress relief brought by natural environments)
- (Carter 71)

Given the eight intelligences, it might be helpful to think of ways that you can manageably and realistically incorporate classroom activities that appeal to the students who, in fact, possess these types of intelligences.

Essentially, the developmental writing class cultivates students' multiple intelligences. First and foremost, developmental writing grounds itself in the developmental of students' verbal-linguistic abilities with the level of writing involved. Given that composing an essay additionally engages students' organizing and sequencing skills, developmental writing strengthens students' logical abilities. The use of more reflective activities, such as journaling, engages students' metacognition (their abilities to think about their learning and writing processes). When students are reflecting upon their process of composing an essay or making a connection with the message of an author, they are strengthening their intrapersonal intelligences. The use of collaboration, moreover, develops students' interpersonal sides. Essentially, activities not foreign to a developmental writing class reflect the multiple intelligences approach.

Meeting the course outcomes for developmental writing is time consuming. Adding the continual evaluation of student writing is even more time consuming. Developmental writing classes may be so labor intensive that you may believe that learning styles falls outside your purview as an instructor, given time constraints. Recall, though, the statistics from chapter 1 about at-risk students and high-risk courses. When it comes time to plan your lessons, consider tapping into the multiple intelligences approach for an activity or two.

Moving Beyond the Lecture—Encouraging More Diverse, Active Learning

As reviewed in chapter 3, effective, but brief, lectures find a place in the developmental writing classroom, especially to set up and conclude a lesson, to interject personal anecdotes, and to explain important concepts. However, a purely lecture format over time fosters more passive learning, which may not yield the best results for at-risk students in high-risk classes. To reach more learners and diversify your course delivery, there are other teaching pedagogies to bear in mind during lesson planning.

Reflective Activities

Reflective activities revolve around opportunities that encourage students to consider the class lesson, activities, and assignments to a variety of degrees—what they have learned and how they might use this newfound information throughout the course, across the curriculum, and into their own lives outside class. Moments of reflection encourage students to explore even in their journals their processes of essay composition. More purposely, journals provide students the opportunity to brainstorm topics for an essay, explore the relevance of a particular reading, or to deliberate, for example, how their thesis sentences connect with their subpoints. In addition to the journal, the one-minute paper (see chapter 3) furnishes students with a short, but effective, way to reflect on a daily class lesson under the direction of their instructors. Traditionally, the one-minute paper would be assigned at the end of class and then handed in to the instructor. While this short assignment serves as a vehicle for students to reflect upon a class lesson, it also provides the instructors some feedback on their students' comprehension of the lesson. Variations of this assignment can even be used at the beginning of a class. Instructors can ask students to review the previous class lesson or ponder some question about a homework assignment, such as a reading. Again, this one-minute (the assignment time frame can be varied) paper at the beginning of class still allows instructors to gauge students' comprehension of class lessons and homework. Whether at the beginning or end of class, the one-minute paper builds in reflection time for students. For instructors, the one-minutes paper acts as an assessment tool, so they themselves can gauge the efficacy of a class lesson. In sum, reflection-based activities engage not only students' verbal-linguistic intelligences but also their intrapersonal sides.

Collaborative Work

As a more learner-centered activity, collaboration certainly develops students' multiple intelligences, and even more, it has been identified as a good practice in undergraduate education. A type of active learning, collaborative learning oftentimes involves group work with two or more participants—students and instructors coming together to learn from one another. As with more active learning, studies suggest that collaborative learning improves students' understanding of course content (Pascarella 102–103). As with many activities and lessons in developmental writing, collaboration bolsters students' verbal (oral and written) skills, as students need to discuss the assignment with each other and even take notes or record the results of their work. Of course, collaboration provides the foundation for interpersonal skill development. Students learn how to work with each other, hopefully allowing each member of a group to assume a role and contribute to the ultimate goal of the group assignment. Along the way, students learn how to negotiate through their discussions allowing each student to speak and problem solve. As noted in chapter 3, in order for collaborative activities to work, instructors need to direct the groups, very clearly drawing from their own logical skills, so students understand their task. Additionally, collaboration potentially calls upon students' bodily-kinesthetic sides by getting them up and about.

Reciprocal Learning

A type of instructional technique, reciprocal learning shores up the engagement of students' differing learning styles. As explained in *How College Affects Students*, reciprocal learning:

> …involves students working in dialogue with classroom teachers to learn a set of strategies for fostering comprehension of textual material. The dialogue is structured to incorporate four crucial components: generating questions, summarizing, clarifying difficult or ambiguous words or ideas, and predicting upcoming content from cues in the material and from prior knowledge of the topic. As they become more adept at using the strategies, students take on more difficult content, and the focus of dialogue shifts from student with teacher to student with student. (Pascarella 111)

Essentially, as a type of active learning, this technique calls upon students' preferred learning styles and may even take them out of their comfort zones. Any dialogue utilizes students' verbal and interpersonal skills. The very nature of critical thinking also taps into students' logical abilities as they broaden their intellectual dexterity by analyzing, questioning, summarizing, and predicting. If any diagrams, pictures, graphs, or drawings are utilized, the teaching will appeal to the more visual learners in class. If there are moments of reflection or connection, students may work on their intrapersonal sides. If students teach other students, they may very likely be drawing upon their bodily-kinesthetic intelligences. Having students singly or in groups, for example, go up to the front of the class to teach a mini lesson demonstrates the reciprocal learning. With appropriate setup, reciprocal learning teaches students how to observe your cues and model your thought processes regarding certain lessons. In turn, students can learn how to teach themselves.

Lessons Appealing to Naturalistic and Musical Intelligences

The multiple intelligences approach to learning offers fruitful ways for instructors to think about how to deliver course content in an interesting, effective manner. This approach encourages instructors to move beyond a purely lecture format. By its very nature, developmental writing classes develop students' verbal-linguistic sides through writing, reading, and discussing. Organizing an essay, following directions, planning a timeline to complete an essay—all engage students' logical intelligences. Developmental writing classes offer rich opportunities for students to sharpen their intrapersonal side through reflection and their interpersonal skills with collaboration. Today, with textbooks filled with colorful pictures and

60

charts, students' visual sides are engaged, as well. Getting students physically involved with their learning—up and about—lends to more bodily-kinesthetic intelligences. How, then, can students with more naturalistic and musical intelligences be involved, or how can students in general be acquainted with the more naturalistic and musical propensities?

Hopefully, a few suggestions will pave the way for more creative consideration and adoption. Within the structure of a class period, students may be introduced to the naturalistic intelligences. Under appropriate circumstances, instructors may conduct a class lesson outside. The lesson itself may have students observe their natural surroundings, noting what they see, hear, smell, and even touch—being attentive to details—in a city, a suburb, or more rural area. Learning to be attentive to detail will certainly help students with brainstorming or developing a paragraph. If venturing outside is not an option, have students look outside a window to note their observations or even have students imagine themselves outside visualizing the sites. Pictures or paintings of a natural setting may be an effective substitute. For an essay, students may identify an important environmental issue and argue a particular point, or they can, for example, compare and contrast effective recycling methods. If viable and appropriate, outside class, students who have naturalistic preferences may be encouraged to find a spot to brainstorm, free write, or even draft an essay. Perhaps, the outdoors may help those students with more naturalistic intelligences to focus.

Students' musical intelligences may also be engaged both inside and outside the classroom. A class lesson could be built around listening to and analyzing a popular song or a student's favorite song. This analysis may serve as the basis for an essay assignment in which students carefully evaluate the messages sent to different audiences. Alternatively, students may compose an essay that compares and/or contrasts songs with similar themes, yet produced in different decades. If the classroom is equipped with DVD/VCR, perhaps students can watch and critique a music video, noting how the production narrates the story. Outside class, students may be encouraged to tap into their musical intelligences by paying more attention to the lyrics of a song, noting, in particular, the diction used. These suggestions simply serve as the base for more creative adoption.

SUMMARY CHART

Learning Style	Effective Learning Strategies/Activities
VERBAL-LINGUISTIC	• Brainstorming, free writing, journaling • Composing essays, revising, editing, proofing • Reading silently and aloud
LOGICAL-MATHEMATICAL	• Organizing essays around logical sequencing • Detecting relationships, such as cause-effect and comparison-contrast • Analyzing reading assignments for main ideas, subpoints, and supporting details • Analyzing sentences to detect grammatical or punctuation errors, such as fragments and comma splices; exploring possible solutions to the grammar and punctuation errors
BODILY-KINESTHETIC	• Teaching a lesson • Editing and proofing the work of other students through peer review • Using a computer to word process an essay or engage in more self-paced class learning
VISUAL-SPATIAL	• Clustering and mapping as types of brainstorming to make connections among different ideas • Reviewing charts, artwork, or pictures to reinforce class lessons or enhance memory
INTERPERSONAL	• Collaborating in pairs or groups within class • Meeting with tutors • Teaching other students through reciprocal learning
INTRAPERSONAL	• Engaging in more metacognitive thinking—thinking about how one learns, goes about composing an essay, detecting error patterns in grammar and punctuation • Journaling • Drafting an essay after careful consideration of a topic
MUSICAL	• Interpreting the lyrics of a song for an essay assignment • Paying attention to the diction within songs to note mispronunciations • Analyzing a music video for a lesson in detail or narration • Using sound and rhythms to remember important concepts
NATURALISTIC	• Discussing or writing about environmental issues • Using the outdoors for a class lesson on detail generation or imagining an outdoor scene for a description paragraph • Interpreting a nature scene from a painting

Ultimately, the different activities used to deliver or reinforce class lessons may call upon several intelligences. Thus, editing and proofing may fall under not only the verbal-linguistic category but also the logical and bodily-kinesthetic ones.

Instructional Activity

Consider activities or assignments that you plan to use, currently use, or might use that incorporate the multiple intelligences. Next to each intelligence, jot down a few notes.

Summary List

1. **Verbal-Linguistic:** _____
2. **Logical-Mathematical:** _____
3. **Bodily-Kinesthetic:** _____
4. **Visual-Spatial:** _____
5. **Interpersonal:** _____
6. **Intrapersonal:** _____
7. **Musical:** _____
8. **Naturalistic:** _____

In brief, the purpose of the summary list is to offer you a space to reflect upon your current teaching practices and to spark ideas for potentially new ones—how you might tap into the different intelligences or learning styles as you deliver your course content and fulfill your course outcomes.

The Use of Technology inside the Classroom

Technology use within the classroom can operate on both a presentational level for the instruction and an interactive level for the students. On a presentational level, Smartboards (interactive white boards), computers, and overhead projectors along with LCD players offer more ways to present materials. When a classroom is technologically equipped, for example, lecture notes, samples of students' essays, or even the observations generated from small group discussion can be projected to the class. Textbook exercises giving students practice in noun-pronoun agreement or consistency in point of view can also be projected in front of the class. If a textbook features online, interactive exercises, the Web site can be accessed and shown to students for a class activity. If the class lesson involves the study of a piece of literature, such as

63

a poem by Gwendolyn Brooks or a novel by Nathaniel Hawthorne, the instructor can access appropriate Web sites featuring the authors—learning about their lives and even touring their homesteads. On a presentational level, technology offers many creative possibilities to present course material. However, using technology persistently as a colorful way to deliver course content, for example through PowerPoint slides, may be another way of simply encouraging more passive learning over time.

Technology, though, is not without its challenges. While technology can potentially enrich learning as an enhancement of the classroom experience, technology does not preclude extra setup time. Before using classroom technology, be sure to review its functions, maybe even scheduling an appointment for a training session. During your review time, you can even identify what computer programs are available to ensure that your own technology is compatible (e.g., your version of Word or PowerPoint matches the classroom computer's version). If the room where you teach is unoccupied before the official start of your class, then you can certainly try to arrive early to set up, so you can ensure that your lesson works with the technology and you do not have to waste valuable class time. The early arrival suggestion is not foolproof. As an instructor, you may be rushing from class to class, building to building, maybe even waiting for the previous class to exit your room, so you can enter. With these scenarios, your time to situate the technology may be nonexistent. There is an alternative. If it takes you several minutes to start the technology, try to locate pockets of time within the class period where students are occupied in independent or small group work. These pockets of time afford you the few minutes that you did not possess before the start of class. To be on the safe side, though, plan an alternative way of presenting the lesson in the event the technology fails to function.

At some colleges, developmental writing classes may be housed in a computer room where each student has access to a computer station. The class itself may be conducted solely in the computer lab, or the class time may be divided between a traditional classroom and the actual computer lab (e.g., one day a week in the traditional classroom and the other day in the computer lab). Either way, the use of a computer lab invites additional consideration of the computer's role in the delivery of course content. On one level, the use of the computer lab may build in conference time with your students. In other words, while your students are drafting their essays on the computer, you could be conferencing with students about their drafts or even updating them about their progress. The lab, essentially, offers more one-on-one time.

On another level, computers, equipped with appropriate technology, can have more of an instructional function in the delivery of class material. There are computer programs where the instructor can control what is displayed or not displayed on the students' computers. For example, if an instructor wants to showcase an essay of a particular student for group discussion, the instructor, through a central computer station, can give the other students access. Conversely, if an instructor needs to block access, such as to the Internet, for a particular student or the entire class, the instructor can perform this function at a central computer station. There are possibilities for integrating the computer into classroom instruction. Many developmental writing texts come with technology. MyWritingLab, for example, offers progressive exercises in grammar and assignments for writing—all of which may be integrated into the computer instruction.

Still on a more comprehensive level, a computer room may be conducive to self-paced learning (e.g., MyWritingLab, MyReadingLab) where the classroom functions more as a lab under the direction and guidance of the instructor. If your class is held in a computer lab, be sure to review the technology in advance. Computer labs come with their advantages, especially for instructors quite excited to use technology in the delivery of class lessons.

There can be challenges, though, especially for the instructor teaching with technology for the first time. Depending on the level of technology involved, careful lesson planning is paramount in deciding the most appropriate ways to integrate the computers. Having a backup lesson is particularly helpful because occasionally equipment fails.

It's a lot to consider. As a developmental writing instructor, your workload is full: the course prep, the classroom lessons, and the evaluation of students' essays continually throughout the semester. Now, there needs to be consideration of the various ways to convey material, even technologically, to students, so they can learn and apply the concepts in class and across the curriculum. As a developmental writing instructor, your placement on the front lines of your students' college educations beckons you to explore teaching methods that work effectively for your students, as you assist in their progression to college composition. To an extent, some interesting insight can be gleaned from Arlo Bates's Introduction to Pearson's *Freshman Composition*:

Dry can composition be only through inadequacy or dullness,—oftener found, I am forced in honesty to add, in teacher than in learner. (Pearson xiv)

Intriguingly, this insight into teaching styles was articulated in 1897.

Helpful Hints

- Take a learning style inventory yourself. Some developmental texts or online supplements may contain inventories for you to try out. Many times, college success texts contain learning style surveys that you can peruse, as well.

- Recognize that as you may have a propensity to a certain style of teaching, students may have a propensity to a certain style of learning. Think about constructing classroom activities that appeal to a variety of students' multiple intelligences.

- Think of techniques that would effectively integrate opportunities for students to reflect upon their learning.

- Include some collaborative activities, so students can problem solve together.

- Experiment with reciprocal learning. With appropriate setup, invite students to teach a mini lesson.

- Consider using technology, if available, to deliver or reinforce a class lesson.

CHAPTER 5

Constructing and Evaluating Assignments for Students

Objectives:

- *To review strategies to create and evaluate assignments*

- *To understand writing portfolios*

- *To explore grading options*

Preparing for class, structuring class lessons, appealing to different learning styles—the planning process of developmental writing continues and culminates with evaluation and assessment. The essay takes center stage in many developmental writing courses, and even the developmental writing levels that focus on the sentence and/or the paragraph do so in preparation for the essay. In *Beyond Tests and Quizzes*, Richard and Barbara Mezeske explain: "Assessment plays a significant role in the learning experience. Not only does it determine their [students'] progression through their program of study, but it also allows them to demonstrate that they have met the learning outcomes…" (Mezeske xviii). Especially for developmental writing, students need to demonstrate learning outcomes (e.g., to learn how to compose an opinion-support essay; to support a main point; to utilize different organizational patterns in an essay) to ensure that they can progress to the next level of writing. It is important, then, to create and evaluate writing assignments that meet the course outcomes to ensure that students are prepared for the next writing course. Where, then, to start?

Defining the Purpose and Outcomes

When creating writing assignments, such as essays, consider purpose and outcomes. Is the assignment designed to give practice? Is the assignment designed to fulfill specific course outcomes that encourage students to learn the steps in forming a thesis or topic sentence, writing an argument, or integrating quotations into an essay using MLA format? Ultimately, by the end of the semester, the course will have addressed a number of learning outcomes, but as you create assignments, consider the outcomes that you would like to meet as you progress to your destination. Over the semester, you will be crafting essay assignments that will build upon a series of skill sets.

Assignment Directions and the Role of Critical Thinking

Writing assignments engage students' critical thinking. Critical thinking holds many definitions, but generally it involves a student's ability to "…identify central issues and assumptions in an argument, recognize important relationships, make correct references from data, deduce conclusions from information or data provided, interpret whether conclusions are warranted based on given data, evaluate evidence or authority, make self-corrections, and solve problems" (reported in Pascarella 156). Research also indicates that some students may possess "the disposition to think critically," which "involves, among other traits, such factors as the inclination to ask challenging questions and follow the reasons and evidence to solve problems wherever they lead, tolerance for new ideas, willingness to use reason and evidence to solve problems, and willingness to see complexity in problems" (reported in Pascarella 156–157). In their very design, writing sequences develop a range in students' critical thinking abilities in a progressive manner.

In fact, the very language (e.g., analyze, synthesize, evaluation) affiliated with critical thinking can be drawn upon to structure writing assignments. In the 1950s, Benjamin Bloom articulated a framework of educational objectives to help instructors teach and engage students in more critical thinking or problem solving. Bloom's taxonomy, as this framework is commonly called, helps instructors create activities, assignments, and assessments that can progress in complexity and difficulty—from lower-order to higher-order thinking. From lower order to higher order, the levels include knowledge, comprehension, application, analysis, synthesis, evaluation. In 2001, with the publication of *Taxonomy of Learning, Teaching, and Assessment: A Revision of Bloom's Taxonomy of Educational Objectives*, the authors L. W. Anderson and D. R. Krathwohl updated the six cognitive domains by changing the names from nouns to action verbs. In addition, some of the domains were updated. For example, the original "knowledge" domain was also updated to "remember"; the original "synthesis" was updated to "analysis"; and the original "evaluate" was updated to "create" (McKeachie 286–287). The following chart classifies the six categories and notes the updating of the original or earlier categories from nouns to verbs.

BLOOM'S TAXONOMY

Original Category (noun)—Revised Category (verb)

Evaluation> Create (higher order) The ability to reorganize elements into new patterns.
Synthesis> Evaluate (higher order) The ability to draw conclusions based on set criteria or standards.
Analysis> Analyze (higher order) The ability to subdivide material parts and connect the parts.
Application> Apply (lower order) The ability to use procedures to solve problems.
Comprehension> Understand (lower order) The ability to construct new meaning by combining new and existing information.
Knowledge> Remember (lower order) The ability to retrieve information.

The definitions are based on the updated taxonomy.

Source: Wilbert. J. McKeachie, *McKeachie's Teaching Tips: Strategies, Research, and Theory for College and University Teachers*. 11th edition (Boston: Houghton Mifflin Company, 2002), 287.

This following list provides a series of additional action verbs that engage critical thinking.

Where and when appropriate, these action verbs can be used in both oral and written directions.

Category	Action Verbs or Directional Cues
Create (higher order)	create, craft, design, generate, plan, prepare, produce, set up
Evaluate (higher order)	check, critique, conclude, evaluate, judge, recommend, revise
Analyze (higher order)	analyze, classify, categorize, compare, contrast, differentiate, examine, explain, group, inquire, interpret, organize, probe, question, structure
Apply (lower order)	apply, calculate, demonstrate, determine, employ, execute, exhibit, illustrate, implement, practice, use
Understand (lower order)	categorize, classify, describe, discuss, exemplify, explain, express, identify, infer, interpret, locate, restate, report, retell, review, summarize
Remember (lower order)	cite, define, enumerate, label, list, name, recall, recognize, repeat, specify, tell

The preceding list of action verbs has been adopted from *A Taxonomy for Learning, Teaching, and Assessing: A Revision of Bloom's Taxonomy of Educational Objectives* (Anderson et al. 31).

To introduce the language of critical thinking to students, compose directions (oral and written) that draw upon the very action verbs associated with critical thinking.

- **Remember**

  Define a fragment. Identify several ways to correct a fragment.

  List several examples that an author uses in an article to support a point.

  Name the three basic parts of an essay.

- **Understand**

  Locate several comma splices within the paragraph.

  Restate the author's point in your own words.

  Categorize and explain different types of genres.

- **Apply**

  Show how the author varies sentence structure to generate interest.

  Use transitions that show contrast.

- **Analyze**

  Classify the types of punctuation errors in the paragraph.

  Arrange the paragraphs according to an emphatic organizational strategy.

Compare and contrast the two authors' articles.

- **Evaluate**

  Evaluate the author's argument.

  Offer a recommendation for improvement.

- **Create**

  Compose a recommendation.

  Revise your essay.

Drawing from the six categories can assist in the creation of assignments, activities, and assessments, especially in the set up or the directions.

Writing Clear Directions

Employing the language of critical thinking in oral and written directions is certainly important, but even more important is articulating the directions coherently. To ensure that your students understand the objectives, be clear with the subject of the assignment and the expectations.

Suggestions for Written Directions

- Provide the due date.
- Use critical thinking terminology in the directions.
- Identify the subject of the essay or explain the assignment.
- List the areas that need to be addressed. For example, if students are new to essay writing, remind them that they need a three-part structure: an introduction with a thesis, topic sentences for each body paragraphs, transitions to link ideas between and within paragraphs, well-developed body paragraphs, and a conclusion. Students can also be reminded to edit and proof their work ensuring that they have grammatically correct sentences and accurate punctuation. Itemize the requirements in a list format.
- Take the time to review the assignment with students in class, so if students have some initial questions about the assignment, they can ask.

In developmental writing, be especially clear and try to stay on task. Even jotting a few notes on the black or white boards will reinforce oral directions and reading skills.

Reading and writing go hand in hand. Some students who place in developmental writing may also place in developmental reading. In developmental reading, students review

71

lessons to improve comprehension, including their comprehension of oral and written directions. In fact, many of the lessons linked with vocabulary, word parts, organizational patterns, and Bloom's taxonomy complement the developmental writing classroom. All in all, be mindful of oral and written directions, as students may still be strengthening their comprehension skills.

The Use of Scaffolding in Directions and Lesson Progression

In essence, Bloom's taxonomy can find utilization in pedagogical techniques called "staffing and scaffolding," which facilitate assignment directions and the progression of lessons. In "Better Student Essays through Staging and Scaffolding Assignments," authors Jon D'Errico and June Griffin note that new students, in particular, struggle with their writing because they lack the most basic knowledge of academic style essays and practice in the higher order of thinking as defined in Bloom's taxonomy. According to D'Errico and Griffin, staging involves the breaking down of an assignment, such as an essay, into a series of tasks or steps that help students move from lower-order to higher-order thinking. Scaffolding provides the structured opportunities to allow students to practice the discrete steps or tasks (D'Errico and Griffin 1–2).

For developmental writing, instructors might provide structured in- and out-of-class opportunities for students to review and practice writing the different parts of an essay before having the students hand in the final version. Instructors can still revisit parts of an essay to give students additional practice in writing. For example, an instructor can review a basic introductory pattern before students hand in their first essay. As the semester progresses, opportunities may arise to revisit the introductory format, perhaps focusing this time on creative lead-in strategies or different ways to construct a thesis once students reach a point where they can handle this additional exploration. In sum, staging and scaffolding provide students time on task, opportunities to learn knowledge, and skill-building practice step by step throughout the writing process.

Responding to Readings

In addition, staging and scaffolding work effectively for integrating reading and reader responses into developmental writing. If, for example, you want your student to write an essay analyzing an article or comparing and contrasting two articles, draw upon staging and scaffolding techniques to reach this objective.

Setup

Students start with being assigned a reading from the course text or a supplement. Given time considerations, the reading can be done at home or in class. In either place, encourage students to apply the SQ3R method (see chapter 3), or at least elements of it, so they engage in more active reading with pen, pencil, or highlighter in hand. In fact, before even discussing the article, you can encourage a student volunteer to walk through the SQ3R process for the class. In addition to the SQ3R, you could consider asking students to share what they know about the general topic of the article before actually discussing the article itself. Together, the SQ3R and the gauging of students' knowledge could serve as a bridge into the discussion.

Remember

- When discussing the reading with students, start talking about the reading by drawing upon the lower-order thinking, even modeling it for your students. You might ask your students what they "recall" or "remember" from the reading. Students can jot down their responses in their notebooks and then share their responses with the class. While the students share their responses, you scribe these responses on the board (reinforcing note taking).

Understand

- Students can then summarize the reading. In fact, a few students could be encouraged to share their summaries. Summaries could even be compared and contrasted.

Apply

- In order to construct a formal summary, students could apply the techniques for structuring a summary learned during another class period. This provides a good activity to reinforce the identification of main ideas from subpoints and details.

Analyze

- Students can be encouraged to break down the article, analyzing its various parts rhetorically and critically. Students can draw from their understanding of an essay format looking for main ideas, subpoints, and types of support or evidence.

Evaluating

- Students can evaluate or judge the types of evidence used. Is the evidence current, relevant, biased? Is the article persuasive? They can make connections with other articles that they may have read or with real-life experience.

Create

- Students can formulate their own opinion of the article, perhaps even making connections with other articles read about the topic. A student's point of view about the article or the subject of the article can then be shaped into an essay that the student composes.

The above example is by no means comprehensive. However, it traces the preliminary steps needed to move students from reading an article to evaluating an article—the steps involved with critical thinking through staging and scaffolding. Drawing from the active learning strategies reviewed in chapter 4, instructors can utilize student groups or pairs to move the class from reading to evaluating. All in all, the steps set the stage for students to create their own opinion essays, perhaps even offering a critique of the reading within their essays. Working with a reading, instructors can continue the sequencing of lessons as they walk students through the essay writing process

Grammar and Punctuation

Sentence-level skills—grammar, punctuation, and mechanics—typically play a significant, yet varied role in developmental writing courses, depending on the levels. By and large, developmental writing texts organize the setup or integration of sentence-level skills quite differently. The following list is by no means all-inclusive, but it does review the basic categories addressed in developmental writing texts.

- **Grammar**: This category typically addresses the eight parts of speech in varying depths and the sentence within the context of conventional usage. On the sentence construction level, texts will include reviews of sentence types, phrases, and clauses along with the identification of typical errors made on the sentence level. Errors, such as run-ons (fused sentences), and comma splices may also be included under this category; however, some texts address fused sentences and comma splices under punctuation. The design of developmental writing texts, including the integration of sentence correctness, does vary.

- **Punctuation**: This category typically addresses commas, colons, semicolons, apostrophes, quoting, and miscellaneous end or internal punctuation.
- **Mechanics**: This category typically includes spelling, capitalization, numbers, and abbreviations.

Within each category, the texts outline appropriate usage or conventions; identify errors linked with grammar, punctuation, and mechanics; and then explain methods of revision of the different errors.

The teaching of sentence-level skills in developmental writing, though, garners much controversy. On the one hand, there are departments that prefer the teaching of grammar, punctuation, and mechanics to be addressed on a one-on-one basis in their college's learning, writing, or tutoring centers. Essentially, the tutorial services may be comprehensive enough to work with students more closely. In fact, some centers may even offer electronic-based programs in which students can largely teach themselves through more self-paced instruction. However, there may be centers that simply lack the resources—human and financial—to support all their students comprehensively.

On the other hand, there are many developmental writing instructors who address grammar, punctuation, and mechanics within and outside the walls of their classrooms. Essentially, there are different levels of developmental writing: the levels primarily focus upon (1) the essay, (2) the paragraph to essay, and (3) the sentence to paragraph. Variations on these levels exist, as well. Within any given developmental writing sequence, the extent of grammar and punctuation instruction grounds itself in the outcomes of the course and the needs of the students. The level of developmental writing that is just below a traditional college composition may need to address fragments, run-ons (fused sentences), comma splices, noun-pronoun agreement—surface errors that can be readily corrected with a lesson and the strengthening of the students' editing and proofing skills. A lower level of developmental writing, though, may need to focus more extensively on the foundation of the English language. In fact, many developmental writing texts targeted for these very foundational levels of developmental writing include chapters on the eight parts of speech and the four basic sentence types—simple, compound, complex, and compound-complex. From the parts of speech and basic sentence construction (phrase and clause types), the textbooks progress to an introduction and review of basic punctuation (apostrophes, commas, colons, semicolons). To address the more wide-ranging needs of their students, some community colleges offer courses or intensive workshops in grammar, punctuation, and mechanics. Like developmental writing, developmental reading experiences a range in levels, and the texts for these classes reflect this range. The more foundational levels of developmental reading address skills at the fourth to sixth grade levels. Developmental writing is no different.

Ultimately, students need to demonstrate their abilities to edit and proof at various stages in the writing process. In *The Bedford Guide for Writing Tutors*, authors Leigh Ryan and Lisa Zimmerelli provide a valuable overview of the student's writing process, especially the points where grammar, punctuation, and mechanics encounter evaluation.

Stages of the Writing Process

Prewriting

- Free writing
- Brainstorming
- Researching
- Observing

Writing

- Creating initial draft

Revising and Editing

- Global revision: improving content, organization, tone
- Sentence-level revision: strengthening and clarifying
- Editing: correcting errors in grammar, punctuation, and mechanics
- Proofreading: looking for typographical errors, omitted words, and other mistakes

(Ryan 12)

Within the writing process itself, there are different stages where students can engage in the address of grammar and punctuation editing and proofing.

Within a developmental writing course, there are different approaches to the teaching of grammar and punctuation, and these approaches certainly reflect the instructors' pedagogies and their assessment of their students' needs. Many developmental writing texts come with exercises either with the text itself or through a supplement, a companion workbook or Web site for students. When necessary, instructors may build in class time or supplement through homework different exercises to help strengthen students' understanding of editing and proofing. However, the key is to transition students from the address of textbook exercises to the actual detection of error patterns within their own writing, thereby sharpening their abilities to apply their newfound knowledge to self-correct when they proof their writing.

Students do need to understand the basic conventions of grammar, punctuation, and mechanics. However, the teaching of these subjects need not be boring. In "Verbing the Noun: Grammar in Action," author Rhoda Janzen reminds her audience that "pedagogic innovation in the grammar classroom" does exist and can exist within your own class (158). Janzen encourages instructors of grammar to tap into active learning. For Janzen, this means getting students physically and creatively involved with their own instruction and learning through games, student presentations, and collaboration. Essentially, if you wanted to tap into some variety, reflect upon the multiple intelligences that include more than the logical and the verbal-linguistic. How might you tap into students' musical or bodily-kinesthetic intelligences? Janzen, for example, composed a game—"The Senator's Cat"—that tapped into the students' rhythms. To the rhythm of clapping, each student would repeat the sentence—"The senator's cat's an ancient cat"; except each student would have to substitute a new adjective in place of "ancient." Essentially, the game segues to the lesson (Janzen 159). This is just one creative way of integrating a brief activity that taps into students' multiple intelligences. The more ways students can take in information, the better their ability to retain the information.

Especially for the unexpected grammar and punctuation challenges that arise, more individualized instruction may be needed either by you, a tutor, or a supplement where the student can dedicate some extra hours for review. When commenting on students' essay drafts or final copies, you can note that a specific grammar review is needed. Your comments or feedback on student writing can be instructive and directive, rather than simply corrective. Engage your students' critical thinking—analysis and evaluation skills. For example, if a student has a stream of fragments, you could ask the student to review his or her notes or text. Next, the student could identify the fragments through careful analysis of the sentences within the essay. Then, the student could practice evaluation skills by offering one or two appropriate ways to transpose the fragment into a complete sentence. To initiate this review process, you could offer brief instruction within the margins of the essay by identifying an example of a fragment and one way to correct it. The example would then serve as a frame of reference for the student, so he or she can revisit the writing and learn how to detect and revise the sentence error. In the end, have your students follow up with you, so the process is complete. The follow-up could be encompassed as part of the revision process or as a separate activity.

More and more, developmental writing texts come with technologies that offer self-paced instruction, as well. Online learning systems, such as MyWritingLab or Catalyst, allow students to go onto the accompanying Web site to practice more sentence-level and basic essay formation skills. MyWritingLab, for example, utilizes a Study Plan Segment. The Study Plan reflects the differing developmental writing levels—from sentence to essay. For the more sentence and paragraph levels, the Study Plan is divided into three sections: Sentence-level Skills, Writing in Practice, and Grammar for ESL practice. Each of the three sections of the study plan is subdivided. If you have a student who could benefit from practice in subject-verb agreement, you could refer your student to the Study Plan tab. Once in the Study Plan, the student clicks on Sentence Level Skills, then the subject-verb tab. Once in the subject-verb site, the study can review a mini lesson on subject-verb agreement and then practice an exercise or two. The goal is to increase the student's competency in order to address the subject-verb error patterns in his or her writing without your assistance. While there are particular types of errors instructors may expect to see within certain levels of developmental writing, there are always some errors that instructors encounter at certain levels which are unexpected. Indeed, supplemental technologies help to individualize students' learning, taking them from where they are to where they need to be for a specific writing level—the very premise of developmental education.

If time permits, you and your students can customize action plans that promote additional practice outside class time. The following is a sample action-study plan template.

MyWritingLab Action-Study Plan

Student Name:_____

Areas to Practice
1. Sentence-Level Skills
  ➢ subject-verb agreement
  ➢ run-on sentences
2. Writing in Steps
  ➢ thesis sentences
3. Grammar Practice for ESL

Under each category, you can identify the areas that the students need to review and practice. As the semester progresses, the action-study plans can be updated to accommodate each student's needs, especially if the focus shifts to more of the essay process. These plans can work as a homework assignment to supplement a traditional classroom or as an in-class assignment in a computer lab setting.

This knowledge of basic conventions that govern the English language is far reaching. Hopefully, students will bring their newfound skills to other classes that include writing—and eventually into the workplace. The more skills students have at their fingertips, the more ways they can communicate, especially for the students who struggle to compose a simple, syntactically correct sentence in the very foundational levels of developmental writing.

Primary Types of Writing Assessments

Portfolio-Based Developmental Writing

The portfolio, a selection of student writing from the semester, is often considered a staple in developmental writing courses. Generally, portfolios can be for both learning and assessment (Reynolds 1). From a learning perspective, the portfolio charts students' progress and reflects their growth as writers: It ultimately evidences the students' writing process (Reynolds 2). Portfolios, though, can also function as an assessment tool in which students showcase their "best works" and are evaluated on the "final product" (Reynolds 2). In fact, some colleges utilize ePortfolio, an electronic portfolio allowing students to showcase their work and even have their work evaluated.

Whether in the hard copy or electronic form, the contents of a portfolio for a developmental writing class can vary. If your department uses the portfolio for developmental writing courses, ask if there are specific guidelines for portfolio content. Basically, the guidelines may outline the types of essays and the minimum number of pages needed for each portfolio. Especially grounded in the writing-as-process philosophy, the portfolio includes the drafts of the students' essays as well as some type of reflective piece. The reflective piece may be a more personal essay or letter to the instructor. An important piece, the reflective essay or letter provides the students a structured opportunity to think about their growth as writers, perhaps acknowledging their strengths and challenges: It allows the students to think metacognitively.

Considered a "best practice" with regard to writing pedagogy, the portfolio grounds itself in three central principles—choice, variety, and reflection (Reynolds 1).

Within guidelines, students select their best writing for the portfolio. The writing oftentimes reflects some diversity in format or style. For example, a portfolio may include several essays, but in particular, the requirements may call for a personal essay, an argumentative essay, and perhaps a reader response. In some cases, the portfolio may include in-class writing, essays that students compose in class under timed circumstances, such as a final exam essay. To give some closure to the process, oftentimes, students will reflect on their progress in class through the portfolio. The reflective piece encourages students to become more aware of themselves as writers. If your department does not have set guidelines for portfolio, then you can certainly establish your own guidelines. For consistency and manageability, portfolios typically adhere to established criteria or guidelines.

In developmental writing, in particular, the portfolio serves as an assessment tool. It provides instructors an opportunity to evaluate students' work more holistically. The holistic approach allows for some flexibility in the evaluation process. Instructors can weigh a number of considerations: organization, development, complexity in critical thinking, control over accurate grammar and punctuation—criteria that would help to document whether or not students met the outcomes for the course. With more holistic grading, instead of assigning a final grade to each essay within the portfolio, the portfolio itself receives the grade.

Portfolio Evaluation Sessions

Some institutions hold formal portfolio evaluation sessions. Essentially, the instructors teaching a specific portfolio-based developmental writing course exchange and evaluate each others' student portfolios. The purpose of the evaluation session is to ensure that each portfolio meets the outcomes for the course. Usually, the exchange takes place on a specific day within the semester when instructors gather to review portfolios. In other cases, one instructor may be paired with another instructor, and the two agree on a time to review portfolios. Still in other cases, an instructor may be given portfolios to review within a time frame and then asked to return them. When you finally review the portfolios, you may be asked to fill out a form noting the portfolio pass or fail with feedback on the portfolio's strengths and challenges. Some forms may actually involve a more comprehensive checklist. Depending on the format for the portfolio evaluation session, some departments may require two readers for each portfolio. If a portfolio is considered borderline pass-fail or is a definite failure, a third reader may be asked to review the portfolio. The additional readers, essentially, are trying to ensure that the portfolio meets the evaluation criteria.

Indeed, portfolio evaluation sessions can be conducted in a variety of ways with each department determining the appropriate format. In many instances, the actual evaluation session takes place at the end of the semester; however, some institutions may, in fact, have a couple of opportunities for exchanges within the semester, depending on the exchange's purpose. Some departments have a mid-semester review to track students' progress or even to fast-track a student through the semester. The fast-tracking allows the student to complete the semester early if course outcomes are met. Depending on the purpose, evaluation sessions hold many forms.

Thus, if you are teaching a portfolio-based developmental writing course, ask for some guidance regarding the format and expectations. If your developmental writing course is not portfolio based, you can consider utilizing one if you prefer more holistic assessment.

Nonportfolio-Based Developmental Writing

Some departments may opt not to use portfolio-based developmental writing courses or may just have select courses within a developmental writing sequence use a portfolio. If the developmental writing course that you have been assigned is not formally portfolio based, your primary method of assessment is still student writing—the essay. Ask your chair, coordinator, or contact for any specific course requirements—minimum number or required essays, minimum length, types of essays, even if there is an exit assessment or final exam essay. These guidelines are designed to help you structure and organize your course. If no guidelines formally exist, you certainly could ask for some examples of best practices within your department or division. Being aware of the variety in current practice will help you formulate your own guidelines for essays. Be aware of the course description and outcomes, as well, because these informational pieces will offer guidance and direction.

The Essay—Stages of Process Writing

Regardless of whether or not the developmental writing course is portfolio based, many instructors—departments—approach the essay as a process taking students from prewriting to drafting to revising to editing and proofing. In fact, many developmental writing texts embrace

81

the essay-as-process approach and will guide students and instructors—chapter by chapter—through the writing process.

In *The Bedford Guide for Writing Tutors*, Leigh Ryan and Lisa Zimmerelli provide a handy overview of the stages of the writing process. In *Writing for Life*, however, D.J. Henry breaks down the stages even further as they relate to developmental writing.

Prewriting

- Decide on topic.
- Determine purpose for writing.
- Gather information.
- Generate details by using clusters, lists, and free writes.
- Organize details into an outline.

Drafting

- Decide on audience.
- Choose format.
- Create introduction, body, and conclusion.

Revising

- Delete details that are not relevant.
- Add details to the ideas that need more support.
- Reorder ideas for clarity.
- Insert transitions between details for a smooth flow of ideas.
- Replace vague or weak words with vivid, strong words.
- Write a new draft if necessary.

Proofreading

- Correct errors, such as fragments, run-ons, shifts in tense, spelling, punctuation, etc.

(Henry 24–25)

Again, developmental writing texts outline the essay writing process as it relates to the different levels in a sequence.

Indeed, this step-by-step process guides the evaluation of student writing, as well. The criteria that you use to evaluate essays at the beginning of the semester may not be as comprehensive as the criteria used to evaluate revisions of essays by the end of the semester. Why is this? The class lesson, like the student writing, progresses throughout the semester. In fact, in the objectives of the assignment, you can let students know that there are certain areas (e.g., basic thesis, topic sentences, overall organization pattern) that will be evaluated in the first draft and additional areas (e.g., paragraph development, complexity in ideas, support, grammar) that will be addressed in the revision. As the semester progresses, students acquire more lessons. Thus, additional criteria may be established or certain criteria may be more heavily weighted within the evaluation of the essay. As the instructor, you can establish your own guidelines or criteria that guide the student writing process and the evaluation of this process.

Formal Evaluation of Student Writing

In essence, the evaluation of essays can be summative and/or formative. Summative evaluation rests generally with the assignment of grades (letter grades, points, checks) as the grades theoretically mark the end of a particular assignment, process, or semester (Reynolds 43). With regard to developmental writing, summative evaluation would denote whether or not the student met the outcomes for the assignment or the course itself. For an outcomes-based course, students generally are judged on the final product

The actual grading of essays or student writing within the course really does vary by department and by individual. Some departments may encourage the assignment of grades to the final draft of the essay or the different stages of the writing process. The grades themselves are individualized. Some departments or individuals prefer letter grades or points. Others may use a check system (check-minus, check, check-plus) to document the students' work, but reserve the final letter grade for the end of the term. In theory, the writing-as-process approach rests on more formative evaluation (i.e., oral or written feedback) even though a final grade has to be given by the end of the course. In reality, many departments or instructors provide some form of grading on student writing throughout the process to ensure that the student understands his or her academic standing within the course. In fact, some colleges may require instructors to submit midterm grades. Essentially, grading provides formal documentation. If you or your department defers the assignment of letter grades on essays or portfolios to the semester's end, be sure that your students are clear on the criteria used to evaluate their work and that they are given adequate feedback on their academic standing until they receive the grades. On occasion, a student will contest a final grade on his or her developmental writing course; therefore, having the documentation will prove important. If you would like to review some approaches to grading, ask for some samples of current practices within your department or division. The samples may, in fact, spark some ideas for your best approach to grading.

In addition to the summative, the evaluation of student writing is formative. Formative evaluation rests with the ongoing review of student writing, as formative evaluation plays a significant role in guiding the students' essay writing processes (Reynolds 48). In formative evaluation, you offer oral and/or written feedback that instructs, guides, and facilitates student writing—prewriting to revision. Your assessment of student writing is more than corrective because your comments help students strengthen their writing and revising. If you require that your students revise their writing—even select pieces from the semester's work—you want to ensure that students are learning from your feedback and are attempting to apply this newfound insight to their revisions.

Feedback on Student Writing

Rubrics

Some instructors find using formal or informal rubrics helpful in the review of student writing at various stages. Formally, instructors may employ a specific form that lists categories for the more global and sentence-level areas that will be evaluated. The global categories may include organization (lead-in strategies, thesis, topic sentences, transition use, organizational patterns, overall unity and coherence, etc.) and development (identifiable points that advance the thesis, support, types of evidence, complexity in idea development, originality, etc.). The more sentence-level elements would concentrate upon grammar and punctuation, as part of the editing and proofing stages. Informally, you may simply comment directly—still addressing the global and the sentence level—on the student's writing or on an attachment. As an instructor, you design the rubric that is appropriate to your lessons and the course's outcomes.

Narrative

Comments on students' writing can be corrective (summative), instructive (formative), or even directive (formative). Historically, the corrective method reinforces the instructor's role as editor or proofreader. Oftentimes, in developmental writing, students need instruction and facilitation, as they are learning or may be relearning the process of writing. Without your guidance, students' growth as writers may be stifled. Oftentimes, with writing courses, it is better to move beyond the corrective into the instructive or directive. Albeit brief, the comments that you provide may offer additional instruction or direct the student to an appropriate resource, such as the class text—to facilitate the students' essay learning processes.

In the *Elements of Teaching Writing*, Katherine Gottschalk and Keith Hjortshoj offer comprehensive advice on structuring feedback to elicit revision. However, two suggestions will prove particularly helpful: describe and ask questions (Gottschalk 70). Specifically, identify or describe the writing's strengths, particularly in relation to the goals of the assignment. In addition to the strengths, identify or describe the areas that still need to be addressed, revisited, or integrated. For example, if the essay's argument shifts focus, let your student know. This identification provides the student direction, so he or she can initiate the revision process. Second, ask questions. For example, you can ask your student to reconsider the types of evidence used to support a point in his/her essay, especially if more pertinent support is needed. The questions will help probe the student's critical thinking process—to develop, to see connections.

Feedback Placement

The placement of comments on student work is also individualized.

- Some instructors prefer margin notes and endnotes; others may prefer either one or the other, not both.

- Some instructors comment on a separate sheet of paper or employ a rubric.

- If instructors prefer recording their comments, they use some type of electronic device.

- With e-mail and course management systems, some instructors, with or without tracking, prefer to type comments into the text of the essay, in the margins, or at the end.

All in all, your comments or feedback need to assist student learning. If there are certain areas for which you will be evaluating, let your students know.

Peer Review

Peer review is an activity that some instructors use to help sharpen students' understanding of the writing process. Some instructors may even require that the peer review be submitted with student portfolios or attached to student essays when submitted. Ultimately, it involves your students sharing their work with each other; however, you would facilitate the activity by pairing or grouping students together and providing specific directions to guide the peer review. Sometimes, instructors may consider peer review as a type of workshop opportunity for their students' writing. To set up the activity, students would need to bring their writing assignments to class. In some cases, the students may be asked to do some writing in class and then bring what they have composed to their pairing or group for review. Once students are in pairs or in groups, they can exchange their drafts of a full essay or even just sections of a draft—depending on the objective of the peer review.

Especially for students who are new to essay writing and group work, peer review can present some challenges. Quite honestly, students may simply be new to essay writing, not to mention peer review: They might not know even what to look for, let alone comment on, in another student's essay. In fact, some students may feel uncomfortable with peer review because they are afraid to share their work, or they feel inadequate in the commenting of another student's work. Still, others may come to the groups unprepared—without their drafts. Even more, a few students may simply view the activity as a chat session rather than a class lesson. Before the actual peer review, remind your students of the classroom expectations or the behavioral decorum statements, as outlined in the syllabus.

If peer review is an activity that you would like to include in your class, there are different ways to address the challenges. One way is to provide some role modeling. Model for your students what you would look for in an essay. If you would like to focus on the structure, review a piece of writing analyzing the structure—thesis, topic sentences, organization, and development. You can ask your students to offer feedback. You could even create more of a "fish bowl" in which you bring together a pair of students for the other students to observe. The students could walk through or demonstrate the essay review process for the other students. Ultimately, you are providing a structured opportunity for students to observe and practice some of the elements of peer review before having them engage in the process.

Another way to offset a challenge with peer review is to provide very clear direction on how the peer review is to be conducted and what specifically each peer is to comment upon with a student's essay. Perhaps, for one peer review, conducted early in the semester, you can have students just focus on evaluating thesis sentences or topic sentences. If you plan to use peer review throughout the term, then certainly the focus of each peer review can expand to include the lessons that have been accumulating throughout the semester about essay writing. Let the focus of the peer review reflect the lessons that you have reviewed in class, so students will have a frame of reference. In fact, you may even distribute a peer review evaluation form, so students will have something concrete from which to work. One final suggestion—while the students are engaging in peer review, closely monitor each group, even reviewing the feedback provided from one student to another. Perhaps you can ask students to share the results, so you can evaluate the content of the feedback to ensure that students are responding appropriately and accurately.

However you chose to facilitate peer review within your class, share with your students the purpose of the review, how they are to interpret the feedback that they receive from other students, and how the review will hone their skills—and ultimately meet the outcomes for the course.

Final Course Grades

As busy as the semester gets with the class lessons, the essay evaluations, and peer editing, instructors must face the inevitable: the tabulation of final course grades for each student. Instructors truly do individualize their grading. Despite this individualization, there still may be departmental or course guidelines of which you need to be aware for developmental writing.

- **Minimum Passing Grades**. Some departments or courses may use the traditional letter grade format—A, B, C, D, or F with plusses and minuses where appropriate. However, some departments or courses may have a specific minimum grade, such as C or C-, as passing. If a student, for example, doesn't pass the course with a C or C-, the student would need to retake the developmental writing course.

- **Final Essay Exams or Portfolios**. Some developmental writing courses may have specific criteria as part of the grade tabulation or the final grade. For example, in order to be eligible to pass a course (each department may define passing differently), students might need to pass a final exam essay or a portfolio.

- **Percentages**. Some departments may require a minimum percentage of the overall final grade assigned to a portfolio or a particular piece of student writing, such as a final exam essay.

- **Pass-Fail Courses**. Some developmental writing courses are strictly pass or fail. Despite the pass-fail grading, instructors still need grading criteria to determine the pass or fail.

Grade Tabulation

Many instructors have their preferred final grade formulation procedures. Some instructors prefer the traditional letter grades with percentages attached to the assessments (essays, portfolio, exams, homework, and class participation). Other instructors still may use a letter grade for the overall final grade, but they employ a point system in their assessment of student work throughout the semester. The points then translate to a specific letter grade.

Sample

The following is an example of a point system employed to tabulate final grades.

- Portfolio—700 points
- Misc. essays-writing—200 points
- Homework, quizzes, etc.—50 points
- Class participation—50 points

Total: 1,000 points for the term

The points would, then, translate to the following letter grades.

- 900-1000 points=A
- 800-899 points=B
- 799-700 points=C
- 699-600 points D
- 599-0 points= F

Sample

The following is another example of a point system used to formulate grades. The points connected to each letter grade can be individualized, or they may be determined by your college.

94-100 = A

93-90 = A-

89-87 = B+

86-84 = B

83-80 = B-

79-77 = C+

76-74 = C

73-70 = C-

69-67 = D+

66-64 = D

63-60 = D-

59-0 = F

If you opt to use a point system, you would formulate the scale that would be appropriate to your developmental writing class. Before, though, the finalization of your own final grade policy, do inquire about any departmental or college policies.

Final Grade Submission

Many colleges utilize online systems to maintain and record student information, including final grades. Be sure to ask about the submitting of final grades, especially with regard to the due date. In fact, colleges may have the due dates noted on published calendars for the semester, or they may e-mail or mail procedural guidelines in advance of the semester's end. If there is a specific electronic procedure, access the site in advance to ensure that any passwords function and that you can navigate the site efficiently. With a deadline looming, you want to ensure that you can enter your grades—and ultimately complete your semester of developmental writing.

At the beginning of the twentieth century, students attending Harvard would have their workload in composition outlined in *Freshman English and Theme Correcting* (1901). What would a freshman student expect to write?: "He is to write twelve fortnightly themes, from three to six pages in length, and on every week day, a theme of not more than one page. Each fortnightly theme, and many of the daily themes, if particularly faulty, must be rewritten, or if fairly successful, revised" (Copeland 3). Interestingly, *Freshman English and Theme Correcting* goes on to detail the actual topics or themes themselves: "Who I am, and why I came to Harvard"; "how to make or do something"; "something learned in a college course;" "an expression of opinion on some topic of interest"; "a criticism of one of the 'required' books recommended"; and "a biographical portrait" (Copeland 4). At the beginning of the twenty-first century, themes and rhetorical modes still serve as a staple in both developmental writing and college composition courses. In fact, even the basic errors in grammar and punctuation, such as run-ons, comma splices, shifts in point of view, and apostrophe misuse, that were identified in *Freshman English and Theme Correcting*, still find a home in both developmental writing and composition. Indeed, the staples persist.

What has changed, though, is the technology. With cell phones, lap tops, and electronic organizers, students are more technologically equipped than ever. Despite their technological savvy, students still place in developmental writing. To address the needs of contemporary students, classrooms appear more learning-centered, as the teaching pedagogies used to deliver content and engage students become more innovative, even tapping into the technological. All in all, you are meaningfully assisting your students—through your teaching, your assignments-assessments, and your evaluation—with skill set development. More immediately, students are purposefully learning the process of creating and organizing unified, coherent essays, which engages and demonstrates their creative and critical thinking. As an instructor, you are helping your students meet the course learning outcomes, so they can progress to the next level of writing. Long term, the skill sets that the students learn in your course will be employed across the curriculum and into their professional lives. From your place on the front lines of your students' college education, you are integrating the traditional with the contemporary.

Helpful Hints

- Pick up a semester calendar published by your college. Oftentimes, holidays and deadlines for withdrawals and final grade submission will be noted.

- Obtain training on any electronic system that allows you to access student or course information, such as class rosters.

- Ask your chair, coordinator, or point person if there are any departmental guidelines (e.g., portfolio criteria, final essay exam requirement) that you need to follow for your developmental writing course.

- Request samples of current departmental practices in essay assignment formats and essay evaluation to help you formulate your own criteria for essay assignments and assessment.

- Review your course text carefully and any instructional technologies that accompany your course text. Sometimes, the technologies may offer more self-paced learning that can assist your students as a supplement to the in-class activity.

- Attend any professional developmental workshops offered by your department or division. These workshops may prove quite helpful in sharing "best practices" or updating you in current departmental guidelines. In fact, some colleges sponsor offices, institutes, or centers for teaching that offer workshops or mentoring opportunities.

- Update your knowledge of technology in the classroom. Some classrooms come equipped with computers and LCD players. If you have been assigned a section of developmental writing in a technologically equipped classroom and you are new to the technology, ask for a review of the equipment.

CHAPTER 6

Making Connections With and For Your Students

Objectives:

- *To understand the role of conferencing*

- *To learn about campus policies*

- *To become familiar with nation-wide initiatives*

Preparing for class, structuring class lessons, appealing to different learners, creating assignments, and evaluating student writing—a routine day in the professional life of a developmental writing instructor documents extraordinary dedication toward students. Yet there are additional reasons determining your role on the front lines of your students' education as imperative. Many of the students sit in your developmental writing courses as first-semester or first-year students. Like your colleagues, you are one of the first instructors your students will have continual contact with in their first, maybe even second semester; thus, knowingly or unknowingly, you assist your students in their transition to college. Even more, for many students, developmental writing serves as a prerequisite for English Composition, a core course for their programs. For so many reasons, making connections with and for your students is of utmost importance.

Student-Instructor Conferences

As a developmental writing instructor, the oral and written feedback that you provide students facilitates their journey through the writing process. Some of this feedback about their writing and class work can take place during conferences. Indeed, the conference, a valuable format to interact with students, is recognized as an effective approach to teaching the writing process, as noted by Thomas Carnicelli in "The Writing Conference: A One-to-One Conversation" (102). However, the use of conferencing with writing courses is actually not new. In fact, as outlined in

Freshman English and Theme-Correcting in Harvard College (1901), instructor-student meetings were built into students' composition studies: "At least four times in each half year—about once a month—each student must hold a conference with his instructor, to review his work and learn his individual needs" (Copeland 3). Today, conferences still offer students a valuable opportunity to meet with instructors outside class time for guidance and more one-on-one instruction. Even more, conferencing about student writing provides you, as an instructor, a structured time to assist students—to engage in a dialogue that will facilitate drafting and revision. According to Carnicelli, the exchange can potentially promote self-learning and responsibility in students (109).

Suggestions for Conferences

- As with all conferences, you can begin with a pleasant greeting and ask your student how you could be of assistance or what brings him or her to visit.

- Listen carefully.

- If the conference is influenced by time constraints, you may need to try to set or establish a clear objective to ensure that your student has the necessary feedback. Some students come with a clear purpose and/or questions about a draft.

- On the other hand, you may have a student who is a bit unsure about how to initiate a conversation with you. On your part, you can ask some general questions about his/her progress in the writing. Even more specifically, you can ask about the topic or thesis. Asking questions can initiate the conversation.

- During the conference, encourage your student to take notes either on the draft itself or in a notebook.

As your conference concludes, you could sum up the areas reviewed, or you can ask your student to sum up the conference. Try to be encouraging and try to conclude the conference with the identification of the next step or area of concentration. Identifying the next step allows your student to know where to start or continue when he or she goes home, to the library, or to the computer lab. Essentially, conferences can be productive teaching opportunities.

However, the conference also provides an opportunity to discuss with students any issues, such as grades or attendance, affecting their classroom performance. To help students stay the course, one-on-one conferencing can be a productive time to review their academic performance. In fact, it is a place where "attributional retraining" can take place. A type of intervention,

93

attributional retraining calls for students to reconsider, with your guidance, what leads to failure and success: It asks students to think about their learning metacognitively (Pascarella 112). For example, some students may have received poor evaluations on their essays and conclude that they are not smart. Your conference hopefully will help the students see that there may have been other causes to the poor evaluations, such as not dedicating enough time to the assignment or focusing on areas that were not relevant. Conversely, you may have students who performed well on assignments. With your guidance, attributional retraining would call for your students to examine why they did well. Some students may conclude that they were incorrectly placed into the course (Pascarella 112). While the misplacement may be accurate for some, you can ask your students to examine carefully what they did in the process of organizing and developing the essay that was effective in obtaining good grades. As a type of intervention, attributional retraining can potentially bolster motivation and goal setting.

Making connections with students outside class time is important. In fact, studies reveal that student-faculty interaction, such as conferencing, influences student learning quite positively (Pascarella 122). Essentially, it enhances students' persistence to next semester and allows them to feel connected to the college. Even an instructor's timely response to a student's e-mail may have a positive impact on that student's persistence (Ishler 38). There are even more benefits to instructor-student interactions: More immediately, students are assisted with their course work; students are updated on their academic status; instructors get to know their students better; instructors may even appear more approachable and supportive; and students, indirectly or directly, are assisted in their transition to college (Ishler 38). With the intensity of the developmental writing curricula, interactions with students may help them stay the course— week by week.

In reality, though, finding conference time with students can be quite challenging, especially when hours and days can be dedicated to evaluating a single set of student essays. No sooner than returning a set of papers to your students, you may be collecting another set. Then, trying to schedule 10-minute conferences with a class of 25 students around these sets of papers poses even more challenges. How then can an instructor, especially one who is part time and lacks appropriate office space, find the time to conference with students?

Given the constraints of time and place, developmental writing instructors conduct conferences with students in a variety of ways.

- Some instructors who do schedule formal conference time outside class try to utilize their office hours. The conferences themselves could be scheduled over the course of a few weeks if needed. Some instructors try to select a key point in the term, such as around midterm, to meet with each student. As an instructor, you need to select the appropriate time that works with your purpose for the conferences and your schedule at the college.

- Some instructors build brief, focused conference time into the class itself. If there is a workshop day or two, instructors can meet with students briefly while the other students are involved in an activity. Given the constraints of class time, the conferences could be scheduled over a few class periods. If workshops are build into your class calendar, then you could even rotate the students with whom you conference to make the scheduling more manageable.

- If they want to have a formal, key point in the term for which to conference with students, some instructors substitute a couple of class periods for the conferences themselves. The classroom is available during your scheduled time. The students, as well, should be available because it is, after all, their class time.

- To meet with students more routinely, some instructors organize group conferences—meeting with several students at a time for an established objective. The conference time could be to approve topics, review thesis sentences, to make up work, to give additional practice exercises, to ensure that the portfolios are organized according to established guidelines, etc.

- Conference time can even be conducted through e-mail or over the phone.

In the end, you as an instructor need to determine the how, the when, and the why of conferencing—the logistics that work manageably and realistically with your schedule.

Campus Policies and Procedures that Connect with the Classroom Experience

Many students come to class prepared and eager to learn. They recognize the importance of mastering the course content, so they can progress to the next level of writing—eventually college composition. As wonderful of a class as you may have, some students will test your patience. Some come to class with no true understanding of acceptable behavioral decorum and, subsequently, will act out in an inappropriate manner. Some students may be disruptive with their chronic talking to other students; some may simply text message their friends and maybe another student in class; and others may be completely disengaged as they focus on homework for another class. These scenarios can manifest even in classrooms that foster the most interactive, dynamic discussions.

In "Civility in the College Classroom," Jennifer L. Schroeder and Harvetta Robertson bring to the forefront the incivility issues plaguing some college classrooms. In fact, the article categorizes a range in incivility: "annoyances [e.g., unacceptable tardiness], classroom terrorism [e.g., dominating class discussion at the expense of others], intimidation of the instructor [e.g., threatening to complain to a department chair or dean if he/she doesn't get what he/she wants], and threats or attacks on a person or person's psyche" (Schroeder and Harvetta 29). To combat the incivility, Schroeder and Harvetta recommend being proactive, being specific with classroom expectations, and acting as a role model (29–30).

As noted in chapter 2, the syllabus provides a structured opportunity to include statements of acceptable classroom behavior, decorum, or expectations—a proactive approach to fostering a civil classroom.

Sample Statement

The classroom is a place of learning. To maximize learning, please do the following:

- Treat each other with respect and consideration.
- Come to class on time and prepared with texts, notebooks, pens, etc.
- Remain focused during class. Eliminate distractive, disruptive behaviors, such as side conversations, cell phone message review, and text messaging.

The statement or list of classroom expectations can be as brief or as comprehensive as you deem appropriate. In fact, if time permits at the beginning of the semester, you can even ask your students to brainstorm a list of behaviors with you—a more learner-centered approach. Once composed, the list can be distributed to students and referenced when necessary throughout the semester. In the end, the statements are designed to foster a safe, productive learning environment.

Indeed, there are certain types of annoyances that can be readily addressed by conferencing with students outside class time or by referencing the classroom expectations statement. Even if you are uncertain about how to handle a situation that is categorized as an annoyance, consult your chair, coordinator, or dean. Even if you met with a student and the student hasn't amended the inappropriate behavior, notify your chair, coordinator, or dean. Keep careful notes because you may have to provide some documentation for your chair or dean to follow up.

However, when a student demonstrates behavior that threatens the safety of you and/or your class, you need to seek immediate assistance from security or an appropriate point person. In a course where students are generating essay after essay, threatening material can even manifest in student writing. If the content of an essay is of concern, immediately alert your chair or coordinator.

Words of Advice

- Day or evening, be aware of your environment—where the emergency phones are located and who is your closest contact person when you are in class.

- Before the start of a semester, take the time to review the college catalog, student handbook, or employee manuals because they may outline campus policies and procedures for handling student issues as they arise.

Campus policies and procedures, as outlined in catalogues, student handbooks, and employee manuals, do directly and indirectly impact you and your teaching in the classroom.

Plagiarism

Campus policies and procedures may also define plagiarism and outline the process for handling cases. Many student handbooks include academic honesty statements, and, in fact, it is worth referencing the campus policies on academic honesty and plagiarism in your syllabus to underscore their seriousness.

The Internet, cell phones, iPods—technology certainly has revolutionized the ways that students practice cheating and plagiarism. Penning notes on the palm of a hand or whispering the answers to other students during an exam appear obsolete in the face of technologically savvy students. Today, students can easily download essays or cut and paste excerpts of sources and claim them as their own. While taking an exam, students can conduct a Web search on cell phones and other electronic sources that provide access to the Internet. Even texting other students the essay questions on a final exam of a multi-sectioned course is feasible. Indeed, opportunities for cheating or plagiarism appear more innovative and pervasive.

And some basic statistics appear to support a climate for cheating. In 1999, *U.S. News and World Report* published an interesting article entitled "The Cheating Game: 'Everyone's Doing It,' From Grade School to Graduate School" in which the authors Carolyn Kleiner and Mary Lord report that "90 percent of college kids believe cheaters never pay the price" (1). In such a climate, it's no wonder that the Center for Academic Integrity at Duke University found that "three-quarters of college students confess to cheating at least once" (Kleiner and Lord 1). A decade later, cheating and plagiarism cease to be in decline, but the research into cheating and plagiarism has taken a curious turn. On August 18, 2008, in "Study Examines the Psychology Behind Students Who Don't Cheat," *ScienceDaily* highlighted interesting research conducted at Ohio State University. The study at Ohio State University sought to identify the personality traits of students who are less likely to engage in cheating. Not surprisingly, students who valued "honesty," "courage," and "empathy" were the least likely to engage in cheating or plagiarism (1). Unfortunately, "Study Examines the Psychology Behind Students Who Don't Cheat" did report that approximately 50 to 80 percent of college students admit to cheating (1). To combat the cheating and plagiarism in general, approximately 20 percent of college professors surveyed in 2003 acknowledged using a plagiarism detection resource, as reported in "A Campus Fad That's Being Copied: Internet Plagiarism Seems on the Rise" by Sara Rimer (1). Despite the complexity with plagiarism and cheating, the developmental writing classrooms have built-in opportunities to discuss academic integrity and ethics in writing.

In some developmental writing courses, particularly those just below college composition, instructors do introduce students to the skill of responding to readings or integrating an outside source into an essay. These types of skills can be accompanied with a lesson explaining academic integrity. In class discussion, some students may be even willing to share some of their own experiences or the experiences that they witnessed in high school or in other college courses. In more probing questions, you can ask students to identify the reasons that motivate people to plagiarize or not to plagiarize. Examples of plagiarism that have made the news could also be incorporated. If students understand plagiarism, they will invest the time into the writing and citing rather than the cutting and pasting.

Lessons on summary, paraphrase, and quotation integration—even on fundamental levels—are rich opportunities to explain the importance of acknowledgement and documentation. Developmental writing texts that do include lessons on summary, paraphrase, and quoting often include comparisons and contrasts of effective and ineffective summaries, paraphrases, and quotations. Provide students the opportunities to practice summarizing, paraphrasing, and quoting, and then integrating these into their essays.

A few additional lessons on plagiarism can emerge. For developmental writing courses that incorporate the very fundamentals of research, lessons involving the evaluation of sources, including those found on the Internet, can be incorporated into a class lesson. Regardless of the level of developmental writing, lessons evaluating the unique writing styles of students can be reviewed. If samples are available in texts, you can share the examples with the students, even creating an activity around the example. As an instructor, you can construct your own examples as an activity or have your students make up some and then evaluate these examples. In the end, you are providing your students opportunities to learn—the process of being a responsible writer—a lesson that can be carried to other classes across the curriculum.

National and Local Initiatives Connecting with Developmental English

Developmental education, which includes developmental writing, has been the focus of many nation-wide initiatives as a means of fostering student success. Many colleges are exploring, studying, and implementing campus-wide initiatives, such as extended orientations, college success courses, intensive advising, self-paced courses, learning communities, and early warning systems, to support their first-semester or first-year students. As an instructor of developmental writing, you may learn about or be asked to participate in classes or activities that connect with some of these initiatives; thus, it is worthwhile to be familiar with some terms.

Early Warning

- *Early warning* is a type of intervention designed to assist students who may be at risk for failing or who may need some assistance from college services. Some colleges have mechanisms in place where you can forward the names of students who are at risk of failing or who could benefit from some assistance to a central office or point person. In turn, the students are contacted to apprise them of their academic status or their instructor's request for them to seek assistance at appropriate college services, such as tutoring. Colleges that utilize early warning formulate their own procedures to guide instructors. Your college may have an electronic system in place that allows you to automatically forward names to an appropriate office at certain points during the term;

other colleges may have a point person contact you after a certain number of weeks to obtain the information; still other colleges may require that you forward names when you deem appropriate. Again, colleges that utilize an early warning have their own systems.

First-Year Experience

- Since the 1970s and early 1980s, colleges and universities have become more aware of the importance of successfully transitioning their students to college and university life. To reaffirm this importance, much research has been, and continues to be, conducted on strengthening student success within the first year. Generally, developmental education has been included in this research because it falls oftentimes within a student's first semester or year. Early warning systems, college success courses, learning communities, and supplemental instruction are just a few examples or initiatives stemming from the first-year experience movement. The National Resource Center for the First-Year Experience and Students in Transition based at the University of South Carolina has long been a leader of this movement. Additional information can be obtained at http://www.sc.edu/fye/. Founded in 1999 and housed in Brevard, North Carolina, the Policy Center on the First Year of College, now the John N. Gardner Institute for Excellence in Undergraduate Education, is another champion in this movement. More information can be located at http://www.jngi.org/.

Information Literacy

- The Association of College and Resource Libraries have approved a set of standards called *Information Literacy Competency Standards for Higher Education.* Comprehensive, the standards are designed, in sum, to develop students' abilities to utilize information within an academic environment. Information literacy crosses all disciplines. At times, colleges may offer class instruction in informational literacy as it connects with students' processing of information—research—into writing. For more information, visit the Association of College and Resource Libraries Web site at http://www.ala.org/ala/mgrps/divs/acrl/standards/informationliteracycompetency.cfm#ildef.

Learning Communities

- Learning communities are pedagogical strategies to delivery course content more holistically. Essentially, course are paired or clustered. For example, a developmental writing and reading course may be paired. A developmental writing, a developmental reading, a developmental math, and a college success course may be clustered. As pairs or clusters, the learning communities register the same cohort of students who come together for a shared learning experience inside and outside the classrooms. In many instances, the learning communities may be united by a theme, an academic level (e.g., developmental courses), or a common activity. Typically, the instructors of the learning communities meet regularly to update each other on student progress and to create shared activities. Based on the research, learning communities, particularly for first-semester or first-year students, provide many benefits: They assist with students' transitions to college, they help students forge connections to the college and with their faculty and peers, and they show how a set of skills in one class can be utilized in another. For instructors, learning communities offer opportunities to work with other instructors to create meaningful, creative approaches to learning. For more information, visit the Washington Center for Improving the Quality of Undergraduate Education at http://www.evergreen.edu/washcenter/home.asp#.

Student Success

- There are many definitions of student success, and the definitions themselves have evolved with the first-year experience movements. Each college may formulate its own definition and measure of student success. In *Challenging and Supporting the First-Year Students*, leaders in the first-year experience movement John N. Gardner, Betsy O. Barefoot, and M. Lee Upcraft note that in its most basic form, student success rests upon the "…successful completion of courses taken in the first year and…[the] continuing enrollment into the second year" (8). The authors emphasize that colleges and universities articulate much more comprehensive definitions.

Supplemental Instruction

- Supplemental instruction (SI) is an initiative often linked with high-risk courses, courses that render a minimum of 30 percent Ds, Fs, or Ws (withdrawals). In its truest form, SI involves sessions held in addition to class time led by student peers (Hurley and Gilbert 1). The supplemental instructor or peer has mastered the course content and has undergone some training to assist the course instructor. The ultimate goal of SI is to increase a student's mastery of course content with more one-on-one or small group sessions outside class time (Pascarella 106). These academic-assistance initiatives come in many variations. In some cases, a tutor or educational assistant, not a student peer, offers additional or supplemental instruction for students. Depending on the structure of the program, the supplemental instructor may assist the teaching in labs or workshops or actually may hold sessions with students outside the designated class time.

Writing Across the Curriculum

- Writing Across the Curriculum (WAC) initiatives rest with the premise that students need to practice and use their writing skill sets beyond their first-year writing courses, as writing reports, essay exams, research papers, etc., become integral components in courses across the disciplines. In sum, students learn to write and write to learn. Some colleges offer formal Writing Across the Curriculum courses. Other colleges may absorb the Writing Across the Curriculum approach in composition. For more information, visit the WAC Clearinghouse at http://wac.colostate.edu/.

Teaching a labor-intensive course, such as developmental writing, consumes quite a bit of your schedule, especially if you are affiliated with more than one institution. Rushing from class to class, building to building, campus to campus—teaching at the college level can feel quite isolating at moments. However, taking the time to forge connections with other faculty and staff is important for you and your students. Essentially, your connections with others provide a supportive network where you can share teaching strategies, give and receive advice on challenging student issues, learn of professional development opportunities, partake of training opportunities, and be apprised of campus events or initiatives that connect with your class—all of which impact your students directly or indirectly. If your department, division, or college offers orientations or professional development workshops, try to participate—for the knowledge gained and the colleagues met.

Remember that your developmental writing course is part of a sequence of courses. Regardless of where your developmental writing course falls within the sequence, you are preparing your students ultimately for college composition. For this reason alone, you are on the front lines of your students' education. Even more, if you are teaching first semester or first-year students, you are on the front lines of your students' college experiences because directly or indirectly, you are helping your students transition to college—even persist to the next semester.

Although at times you may feel that teaching at college occurs in isolation, your teaching is definitely part of a much more comprehensive educational network locally and nationally. Try to stay connected with your college—for you and your students. The conversations alone can be quite valuable.

<u>Helpful Hints</u>

- Consider how you might integrate brief conferences with students into your office hours or classroom workshops. Given your teaching load and the number of students, be realistic about what you can reasonably manage in a semester.

- Review college catalogues and/or student handbooks because they typically outline policies and procedures regarding plagiarism and student conduct.

- Familiarize yourself with campus contacts in case you need assistance.

- Try to attend department, division, or college-wide workshops or orientations for the information and the contacts.

- Converse with other instructors, as they can offer a supportive network.

- Be open to initiatives that connect with the first-year experience or student success.

CHAPTER 7

Professional Development and Resources

Objectives:

- *To understand the role of professional development*

- *To learn about professional organizations*

- *To review tips and suggestions for enhancing the curriculum vitae (CV)*

In the Introduction to Henry Pearson's *Freshman Composition (1897)*, Professor Arlo Bates draws a rather compelling conclusion about the connections among the students, the instructor, and the course text:

> The success of any teacher of course depends less upon the text-book than upon the personal equation. The ideal text-book is a volume which furnishes necessary facts and the best system of mastering and arranging them, but which leaves to the teacher the part of presenting them and to the pupil the task of grasping and assimilating. No teacher makes a student master the difficult art of composition. He can at most but direct and assist, so that the efforts of the learner shall be exercised to the best advantage. (xi)

Indeed, Professor Bates's rather prolific insight still resonates today. Studies often indicate that interactions between instructor and student can potentially influence whether or not a student meets academic goals and persists to the next semester or year. Even the Community College Survey of Student Engagement (CCSSE) sees fit to pose a question to students about their interactions with instructors, as the CCSSE reaffirms the profound impact that instructors can potentially have on their students' lives. Essentially, the quality of instruction rests with more than the textbook. However, many factors impact the "personal equation," as Professor Bates dubs the interactions between instructor and student. One such factor is professional development.

Teaching developmental writing is an important responsibility. Oftentimes, developmental courses, including developmental writing, fall within the category of at-risk

104

courses—courses in which there are 30 percent or more D, F, or W grades. Oftentimes, students who sit in developmental courses are first-semester or first-year students. To prepare to teach developmental writing, to bolster your understanding of developmental education, to learn to work with student challenges, and to invigorate your teaching pedagogies, it is important to school yourself with professional development.

Professional development assumes many forms. On the local level, your college or department may offer workshops, conferences, or training opportunities to indoctrinate its instructors into its academic environment. If your college offers training in their technologies, especially to assist you in completing the more administrative obligations, try to attend. With e-mail, course management systems, and electronic grade submissions, technology occupies a significant space in an instructor's day. In fact, two-year public colleges hold the lead over four-year public and private institutions in the incorporation of hands-on technologies for instructors to use in their developmental courses (Pasad 5). With computers and other technologies integrated into or structuring the classroom experience, it is important to update skill sets for teaching. In fact, your department or college may have an office, center, or Web site for teaching and/or adjuncts where you can learn not only about local, but also national, professional developmental opportunities.

On a national level, colleges, publishers, and organizations linked with developmental English or English in general host workshops and conferences. Learn more about professional organizations, such as the National Association for Developmental Education (NADE), because oftentimes these organizations sponsor or host workshops, conferences, and lectures. Even the publishers of your course texts hold national conferences that you can attend or where you can perhaps make a presentation. Conferences, though, can accrue costs with the fees, travel, and hotel accommodations. To defer costs, some colleges will contribute funds toward professional development for part-time instructors. Inquire with your human resource department or department chair about professional development funding procedures. When identifying a particular national conference of interest, inquire about fee deductions or waivers, as well. Part-time instructors may be eligible to attend at a reduced rate or at least apply for a fee waiver. Many organizations understand firsthand the costs affiliated with attendance, so they may offer a fee waiver for instructors who are selected to present a paper or host a session. In the end, the knowledge gained and the ideas sparked directly or indirectly influence your teaching of developmental writing and your interactions with your students.

Journals, Web Sites, and Professional Organizations

To stay current or to learn more about your field, the following list provides some helpful links to national conference sites, journals, and associations. Many of these feature additional links to related sites and valuable resources.

Conferences

- **Conference on College Composition and Communications**
  http://www.ncte.org/cccc/ccc
- **National Association of Developmental Education (NADE) Conference**
  http://www.nade.net/conferences/conferences.html
- **Two-Year College English Association (TYCA) Regions-Conferences**

    TYCA Midwest

    http://www.tycamw.org/

    TYCA Pacific Northwest

    http://www.tyca-pnw.org/

    TYCA West

    http://tycawest.org/

    TYCA Pacific Coast

    http://ecctyc.org/

    TYCA Southwest

    http://tycasw.org/

    TYCA Northeast

    http://www.tycanortheast.org/

    TYCA Southeast

    http://www.tycasoutheast.org/

Journals, Magazines, and Newspapers

- *The Adjunct Advocate*

  http://adjunctadvocate.com/magazine/

- *Chronicle of Higher Education*

  http://chronicle.com/

- *Chronicle of Higher Education-Chronicle Careers*

  http://chronicle.com/jobs/

- *College Composition and Communication*

  http://www.ncte.org/cccc/ccc

- *Journal of Developmental Education*

  http://www.ncde.appstate.edu/publications/jde/

- *Teaching English in the Two-Year College*

  http://www.ncte.org/journals/tetyc/issues/v36-2

- *The Teaching Professor*

  http://www.teachingprofessor.com/newsletter/index.html

- *Tomorrow's Professor (sm) E-mail Newsletter*, Sponsored by the Stanford Center for Teaching and Learning

  http://cgi.stanford.edu/~dept-ctl/cgi-bin/tomprof/postings.php

Grants

- **Conference on College Composition and Communications**

  http://www.ncte.org/cccc/conv

  National Association for Developmental Education (NADE)

  http://www.nade.net/NADEdocuments/Awards_Grants_and_Scholarships.pdf

- **National Council of Teachers of English**

  http://www.ncte.org/grants

Web Sites

Community Colleges

- **American Association of Community Colleges**

  http://www.aacc.nche.edu/Pages/default.aspx

- **Community College Survey of Student Engagement**

    http://www.ccsse.org/

Developmental Education

- **National Association of Developmental Education (NADE)**

    http://www.nade.net/

- **National Center for Developmental Education (NCDE)**

    http://www.ncde.appstate.edu

English

- **College Reading and Learning Association**

    http://crla.net/

- **Two-Year College English Association**

    http://www.ncte.org/tyca

- **Modern Language Association**

    http://www.mla.org/

- **National Council of Teachers of English**

    http://www.ncte.org/

- **Writing Across the Curriculum Clearinghouse**

    http://wac.colostate.edu/

First Year

- **National Resource Center for the First-Year Experience and Students in Transition**

    http://www.sc.edu/fye/

- **John N. Gardner Institute for Excellence in Undergraduate Education (an outgrowth of the Policy Center on the First Year of College)**
    http://www.jngi.org/

Learning Communities

- **Washington Center for Improving the Quality of Undergraduate Education**

    http://www.evergreen.edu/washcenter/home.asp

Tips and Suggestions for Enhancing the *CV* and Your Employability

Some part-time instructors of Developmental English seek to move into full-time teaching positions. If you are considering applying for a full-time faculty position in developmental English, there are some suggestions that you may consider to enhance your *curriculum vitae* or *CV*, a comprehensive version of a résumé:

- Continue to teach as an adjunct if possible. The experience gained accumulates on your *CV*. If you are looking to specialize in either developmental writing or reading, request those courses.

- Peruse employment sites. If you are interested in a full-time position, check out college Web sites, particularly the human resource link. Oftentimes, the college or post-secondary education links at some state sites will list available positions. *The Chronicle of Higher Education* and the Web sites of some professional organizations will post job listings, as well. Even some graduate departments may offer some assistance in the job search. Actually, the job postings can be quite insightful because they sometimes list key areas that are being sought by colleges. Some of your professional development may be tailored, so you can strengthen areas in demand.

- Read. Check out the college library periodical room. There may be a particular developmental education or English journal of interest. Some colleges have an office or center for teaching or professional development. This office or center may have professional development materials, such as a subscription to the *Teaching Professor*, a newsletter that reports on teaching pedagogies and best practices. Your interview and teaching will be much more informed.

- Attend department, division, or college-wide workshops. Your attendance allows you to gain knowledge, meet colleagues, and demonstrate your genuine commitment to teaching.

- Look into a state-wide or national conference. Conferences can be quite expensive, especially if there is no funding from your college. If no funding is available and your resources are limited, you might consider attending some local workshops that may be of no charge. Advertisements of these local conferences may be posted in your department or division. Ask a colleague within your department if he or she knows of any local workshops or conferences that may be of interest. There may even be a link serve that you might join. If you are interested in attending a national workshop, investigate ones of interest that might work with your financial resources. Many of the national conferences rotate their meeting locations each year, so at some point, the conference may come closer to your home state. Visit the national organization or conference sites to learn of upcoming meeting dates and locations.

- Demonstrate knowledge of your college environment. If you have been invited for an interview for either a part-time or full-time position, demonstrate knowledge of the college. Visit the Web site. Review the course catalogue (electronic or print), so you are familiar with the developmental writing courses and the English sequence. Ask thoughtful questions about the college, the students enrolling in developmental English, the responsibilities accompanying the teaching, and any special requirements of developmental English courses.

- Try to stand out in a positive, professional manner. In addition to your knowledge base, try to engage in activities that will be distinguishing. Consider volunteering. Ask about innovative teaching opportunities of which you may participate. Many colleges offer learning communities, computer-assisted instruction, and summer programs that will bolster your teaching experience.

- Write. If you are interested in publishing, investigate some newsletters, newspapers, or journals that match your interests. Visit their Web sites. Typically, the Web sites or the print materials outline submission guidelines.

- Compile a teaching and/or professional development portfolio. In brief, a teaching portfolio is a collection of materials documenting your accomplishments in teaching. Some portfolios might also feature documentation of professional development. On a personal level, the portfolio tracks and showcases accomplishments. On a professional level, the portfolio evidences teaching contributions to a hiring committee. In *The Teaching Portfolio: A Practical Guide to Improved Performance and Promotion and Tenure Decisions*, author Peter Seldin outlines steps to consider when compiling a teaching portfolio. First, plan. Give considerations to purpose and audience. Second, summarize teaching and teaching-related responsibilities. Identify the courses taught (where and when), even the levels. If you served as a tutor, an educational assistant, or in a role connected to education, document (where, when). Third, describe your teaching goals, philosophy, and pedagogies. More reflective, this piece allows you to articulate your very teaching foundation. Fourth, select pieces for your portfolio.

Sample syllabi, sample assignments, sample evaluations of student work, sample student evaluations, copies of classroom observations or evaluations, letters of thanks or recognitions, awards or acknowledgements—all are possibilities. Some instructors may even include a DVD of their actual classroom teaching. For those who would like to include professional development, provide copies of presentations and/or publications. Quite comprehensively, Seldin details additional steps to take in the compilation of a portfolio, but the crux of the progress rests with the planning, the summarizing, the describing, and the selecting. Additional statements or reflections on each item may be included. In the end, the materials need to be organized and housed in a reader-friendly portfolio (Seldin 7–8).

In many cases, both part-time and full-time applicants are asked to submit a portfolio of their work—sample syllabi, sample assignments, course evaluations, self-assessments, statement of teaching philosophy, sample publications—along with their *CV*. For more information about the teaching portfolio, consult *The Teaching Portfolio: A Practical Guide to Improved Performance and Promotion and Tenure Decisions* by Peter Seldin.

In sum, for those seeking to move from part-time to full-time employment as an English or developmental English instructor, be sure to meet the minimum educational requirements, work toward building a *CV*, shore up pedagogical knowledge, and be very prepared in the interview. Ultimately, prove that you can fulfill the position's responsibilities and still bring something special to the students, the department, and the college.

"The success of any teacher of course depends less upon the text-book than upon the personal equation," penned Professor Arlo Bates in the Introduction to *Freshman Composition* published just before the turn of the twentieth century. In essence, Bates notes that the teacher brings learning to life—energizes the classroom, facilitates instruction, and guides the student. One effective way to enhance your teaching of developmental writing and enrich your understanding of your students is to engage in professional development. Professional development assumes many forms—more informal or formal, more local or national. Be on the look out for opportunities that match your interests and fit manageably within your busy schedule. If you are interested in a full-time position, be alert, especially to the community colleges.

Given the current state of the economy, the community college offers an affordable, quality filled education for a diversity of students. Indeed, high-quality, knowledgeable, dedicated instructors will be needed to meet this demand. However, competition for full-time, tenure track positions is intense. As reported by the U.S. Department of Labor's Bureau of Labor Statistics, employment for postsecondary teachers is expected to grow between 2006 and 2016 by as much as 23 percent. Although growth is expected, many openings may be for part-time or nontenure-track positions. Again, professional development is one effective way to prepare for class and the competition for full-time positions. Even more, professional development allows you to stay current in your role on the front lines of your students' education in developmental writing.

Helpful Hints

- Attend technology or resource training sessions offered by your college. The sessions will help you utilize the technologies connected with your teaching responsibilities.
- Participate in local professional development workshops where you can update your knowledge base of innovative teaching pedagogies and ultimately energize your teaching.
- Investigate the availability of professional development funding, especially for state-wide or national conferences, at your college.
- Ask about information or resources specifically for adjuncts. Some colleges have adjunct manuals, Web sites, centers, or associations that are designed to keep adjunct instructors informed about campus policies, teaching strategies, etc.
- Inquire about in-class observations. Not all colleges routinely evaluate their adjunct faculty because they lack the human resources. However, inquire about your department or division. The opportunity to be evaluated or observed in the classroom fosters a greater discussion about your teaching.

- Check out your college library's periodical room or data base for periodicals in your field.
- Visit the Web sites of national organizations or their local chapters. Oftentimes, the sites have a wealth of literature to peruse.

CHAPTER 8

The Importance of the Developmental Writing Instructor

Objective:

- *To recap the role of Developmental Writing Instructors*

At most community colleges, 65 percent of faculty members who teach developmental courses are part time (Boylan 55). While the percentages may vary from college to college, 65 percent occupies a significant place nationwide. Even more, 30 percent of adjunct instructors nationwide teach three or more classes in a given semester (Green 29). For instructors of developmental writing, the classes fill, and the weeks meet with continuous prep and paper evaluation. Given the nature of teaching, the bustle of any given semester begins before the first day of class and ends after final grades come due. As an instructor, you play a significant role within not only your department but also your college.

Indeed, more than a few students depend upon you for assistance, as well. Developmental writing courses, as other developmental English courses, serve a growing number of students entering community colleges across the nation. More precisely, 65 percent of first-time community college students enroll in at least one developmental-level course (Roueshe 19). In fact, 98 percent of the public-two year colleges provide developmental education courses in writing, reading, and/or mathematics, as reported in *Education Statistics Quarterly* (Parsad and Lewis 1). In the *Second National Survey of First Year Academic Practices*, the Policy Center on the First Year of College (now known as the John N. Gardner Institute for Excellence in Undergraduate Education) found that 98.57 percent of the two-year colleges surveyed (public and private) offer developmental English, more than likely writing, and 95.94 percent of the two-year colleges provided developmental reading. Not surprisingly, in comparison to four-year institutions, two-year public colleges had a higher number of incoming freshmen registering for developmental courses (Parsad and Lewis 3). Most four- and two-year institutions across the

114

nation—up to 88 percent—attach some restrictions on college-level courses for students placing into developmental education (Parsad and Lewis 5).

For some colleges, these restrictions come in the form of prerequisites. For example, in order for a student to enroll in an Introduction to Psychology course at some institutions, the student might need a corequisite or prerequisite of English Composition 101, especially if the psychology course requires the reading, writing, and research skill sets reflected at the college composition level. If a student sits in a class with intense reading, required writing, and maybe even a research component, the student requires the listening, writing, reading, and researching levels to understand and apply the course work. At other institutions, students placing in developmental courses may need to complete their developmental course requirements before actually registering for college-level courses, usually designated as 101 or above (the course numbering systems do vary across the nation). The developmental courses, including writing, are designed to assist students in the learning, relearning, and practicing of vital skills needed for other college courses.

Community colleges open their doors to a diversity of students with a range in skill levels. For those students placing into developmental writing, completing developmental writing proves critical. For the short term, students who place into developmental writing need to pass developmental writing in order to enroll in college composition. For the long term, students need college composition oftentimes to fulfill their degree requirements for graduation. Ideally, students will take their newfound writing and reading skill sets across the curriculum and into their workplaces—their future careers.

It's not that easy, though. On the one hand, some students who place into developmental writing require a refresher and some skill set development to move on to college composition quite successfully within a semester. On the other hand, some students need to revisit the very foundations of the English language; as a result, they may need three, maybe even four, semesters of developmental writing. After a series of unsuccessful attempts to pass developmental writing, some students may be encouraged or required to seek counsel from an academic advisor, especially within colleges that may place restrictions on the length of time to complete developmental courses. In fact, many instructors may not even realize that they are inheriting—in some cases—a tradition of at-risk courses. Firsthand, the instructor of developmental writing witnesses the struggles of students confronting the challenges of

115

college—the reality of learning or relearning the very rudiments of the English language. Even more, the instructor of developmental writing comes to realize that some of the more traditional methods of teaching fail with students who grapple with the verbal-linguistic and the mathematical-logical.

Indeed, semester after semester, states and their community colleges face the reality of increasing enrollment in developmental courses and the fledgling retention, the ability to retain students to their next semester, their next academic year—the time it takes to graduate and/or transfer to a four-year institution. To address the challenge of retention, many colleges are implementing campus-wide initiatives with developmental education to assist students with their transition to college and their ability to master course content. In their classrooms, many instructors of developmental English heed the call to practice their most effective ways of delivering course content to ensure that students meet the course outcomes.

Much goes into the teaching of developmental writing—learning about developmental education itself; preparing for class; teaching developmental writing content; appealing to different learners; constructing and evaluating assignments; making connections for yourself and your students; and even developing professionally to inform and energize your classroom. There are, unfortunately, a few in academe who still place little value on instructors—full- and part-time—of developmental education, and this lack of value manifests itself through the lack of adequate support on many fronts.

Yet, the instructor of developmental writing holds many imperative roles. For the college, you educate many first-year students as you help the college fulfill its mission to the community. Fortunately, many colleges do recognize this extraordinary commitment and do attempt to offer a supportive teaching and learning environment. For your division or department, you are imperative, not only for your agreement to teach the staple course of developmental writing, but also for your role in helping students progress in the writing sequence. For students who accept the offer to learn, you are imperative in helping them meet the course outcomes—and so much more. Indeed, for accepting the developmental writing course assignment with such fervent commitment, you are truly commended. With that, this guide offers some assistance—to fortify your role on the front lines of your students' college education.

Helpful Hints

- Take an active role in learning more about your college, including its very mission, because as an instructor, you help the college fulfill its responsibility to the community.

- Review college print and electronic materials because they offer a wealth of information. As an instructor, you may be the first line of contact for your students.

- Reach out to other instructors of developmental writing. Sharing information can be helpful and supportive of your teaching experience. Some colleges even have centers, Web sites, or manuals designed to assist the part-time instructor.

- Update your own skill sets for teaching. Combine creativity with practicality in the classroom.

- Familiarize yourself with the college's technological resources, as some administrative functions are done electronically.

- Review your course outcomes and descriptions carefully as they will indicate areas of instructional focus.

- Be sure to fulfill any department, division, or course requirements, as developmental writing is generally part of a sequence that progresses students to college composition.

- Try to prepare your course syllabus in advance. Questions may arise in the planning process. If you are assigned a course within days—or hours—of the semester's start date, try to get your questions addressed as soon as possible.

- Interact with your students. Your connections make a difference.

- Respect the mission of developmental education and the student whom it serves.

Works Cited

Alliance for Excellent Education. "Making Writing Instruction a Priority in America's Middle and High Schools (Policy Brief)." April 2007. 1-7. <http://www.all4ed.org.>

American Association of Community Colleges. "Fast Facts 2009." January 30, 2010. <http://www.aacc.nche.edu/AboutCC/Pages/fastfacts.aspx>.

Anderson, Lorin W., David R. Krathwohl, Peter W. Airasian, Kathleen A. Cruikshank, Richard E. Mayer, Paul R. Pintrich, James Raths, and Merlin C. Wittrock, eds. *A Taxonomy for Learning, Teaching, and Assessing: A Revision of Bloom's Taxonomy of Educational Objectives. Abridged Edition.* New York: Longman, 2001.

Arendale, David. "Then and Now: The Early Years of Developmental Education." *Researching and Teaching in Developmental Education* 18.2 Number (2002): 5-23.

Astin, Alexander W. *What Matters in College? Four Critical Years Revisited.* San Francisco: Jossey-Bass Publishers, 1993.

Bates, Arlo. Introduction. *Freshman Composition.* By Henry G. Pearson. Boston: D.C. Heath & Co., Publishers, 1897. ix-xiv.

Bok, D. *Our Underachieving Colleges: A Candid Look at How Students Learn and Why They Should Be Learning More.* New Jersey: Princeton University Press, 2006.

Boylan, Hunter. *What Works: Research-Based Practices in Developmental Education.* Boone, North Carolina: National Center for Developmental Education at Appalachian State University, 2002.

Carnicelli, Thomas A. "The Writing Conference: A One-to-One Conversation." Eds. T. Donovan and B. McClelland. *Eight Approaches to Teaching Writing.* Urbana, IL: National Council of Teachers of English, 1980. 101-131.

Carter, Carol, Joyce Bishop, Judy Block, and Sarah Lyman Kravits. *Keys to Effective Learning: Developing Powerful Habits of Mind.* 5th edition. New York: Prentice Hall, 2008.

Casazza, Martha E., and Sharon L. Silverman. *Learning Assistance and Developmental Education: A Guide to Effective Practice.* San Francisco: Jossey-Bass Publishers, 1996.

Cohen, Margaret W., Barbara J. Millis, and Judith Grunert O'Brien. *The Course Syllabus: A Learner-Centered Approach.* 2nd edition. San Francisco: Jossey-Bass, 2008.

Compton, Jonathan, Elizabeth Cox, and Frankie Santos Laanan. "Adult Learners in Transition." *Understanding Students in Transition: Trends and Issues.* Ed. Frankie Santos Laanan. *New Directions in Student Services.* Number 114. San Francisco: Jossey-Bass. Summer 2006. 73-80.

Copeland, Charles Townsend, and Henry Milner Rideout. *Freshman English and Theme-Correcting in Harvard College.* Boston: Silver, Burdett and Company, 1901.

D'Errico, Jon, and June Griffin. "*Better Student Essays through Staging and Scaffolding.*" *Teaching Concerns: A Newsletter for Faculty and Teaching Assistants.* Spring 2001. 1-2. <http://trc.virginia.edu/Publications/Teaching_Concerns/Spring_2001/TC_Spring_2001_DErrico_Griffin.htm>

Gardner, John N., Betsy O. Barefoot, and M. Lee Upcraft. *Challenging and Supporting The First-Year Student.* San Francisco: Jossey-Bass, 2004.

Gottschalk, Katherine, and Keith Hjortshoj. *The Elements of Teaching Writing: A Resource for Instructors in All Disciplines.* Boston: Bedford/St. Martin's, 2004.

Green, Donald W. "Adjunct Faculty and the Continuing Quest for Quality." *The Current Landscape and Changing Perspectives of Part-Time Faculty. New Directions for Community Colleges*. Ed. Richard L. Wagoner. Number 140. Winter 2007. San Francisco: Jossey-Bass. 29-38.

Henry, D. J. *Writing for Life*. New York: Prentice Hall, 2007.

Hurley, Maureen, and Melinda Gilbert. "Basic Supplemental Instruction Model." *Supplemental Instruction: Improving First-Year Student Success in High Risk Courses*. Monograph #7. 3rd edition. Eds. Marion E. Stone and Glen Jacobs. Columbia, SC: University of South Carolina, National Resource Center for The First Year Experience and Students in Transition. 2008. 1-9.

Ishler, Jennifer L. Crissman, and M. Lee Upcraft. "The Keys to First-Year Student Persistence." Eds. John N. Gardner, M. Lee Upcraft, and Betsy O. Barefoot. *Challenging and Supporting The First-Year Student*. San Francisco: Jossey-Bass, 2004. 27-45.

Janzen, Rhoda. "Verbing the Noun: Grammar in Action." *Beyond Tests and Quizzes: Creative Assessments in the College Classroom*. Eds. Richard J. Mezeske and Barbara A. Mezeske. San Francisco: Jossey Bass, 2007. 152-169.

John N. Gardner Institute for Excellence in Undergraduate Education (formerly Policy Center on the First Year of College). *Second National Survey of First-Year Academic Practices, 2002*. January 29, 2010.
<http://www.jngi.org/uploads/File/2002_2nd_Nat_Survey_Responses_ALL.pdf.>

Kleiner, Carolyn, and Mary Lord. "The Cheating Game: 'Everyone's Doing It,' from Grade School to Graduate School." *U.S. News and World Report*. Posted Nov. 14, 1999. 1-8. <http://www.usnews.com/usnews/culture/articles/991122/archive_002427.htm>.

Kolb, Alice, and David D. "Assessment Tools." *Experience Based Learning Systems*. Nov. 2007.< http://www.learningfromexperience.com/.>

Krech, Patsy. "Developing Writers Using Technology." *2001: A Developmental Odyssey*. Ed. Jeanne. L. Higbee. Warrensburg, MO: NADE, 2001.

Lester, Jaime. "Who Will Serve in the Future? The New Student in Transition." *Understanding Students in Transition: Trends and Issues*. Ed. Frankie Santos Laanan. *New Directions in Student Services*. Number 114. San Francisco: Jossey-Bass. Summer 2006. 47-61.

Marti, Eduardo J. "Adjunct Faculty as Valued Members of the Academy." *Adjunct Faculty in Community Colleges*. Ed. Desna Wallin. Boston: Anker Publishing, 2005. 43-51.

Maxwell, Martha. *Improving Student Learning Skills*. Clearwater, FL: H & H Publishing Company, 1997.

McCabe, Robert H. *Yes We Can!: A Community College Guide for Developing America's Underprepared*. Phoenix, Arizona: League for Innovation in the Community College and American Association of Community Colleges, 2003.

McKeachie, Wilbert J. *Teaching Tips: Strategies, Research, and Theory for College and University Teachers*. 11th edition. New York: Houghton Mifflin, 2002.

Mezeske, Richard J., and Barbara A. Mezeske, eds. *Beyond Tests and Quizzes. Creative Assessments in the College Classroom*. San Francisco: Jossey-Bass, 2008.

National Association of Developmental Education (NADE). "2009 Fact Sheet." January 30, 2010. <http://www.nade.net/NADEdocuments/FactSheet.pdf.>

Nelson, Robert. "Establishing Personal Management Training in Developmental Education and First-Year Curricula." *Developmental Education: Preparing Successful College Students*. Eds. Jeanne L. Higbee and Patricia L. Dwinell. Monograph Series Number 24. South Carolina: University of South Carolina, National Resource Center for The First-Year Experience & Students in Transition, 1998. 169-184.

Parsad, Basmat, and Laurie Lewis. "Remedial Education at Degree-Granting Postsecondary Institutions in Fall 2000." *Education Statistics Quarterly* 5.4 (Fall 2000) 1-6.
<http://nces.ed.gov/programs/quarterly/Vol_5/5_4/4_4.asp.>

Pascarella, Ernest. T., and Patrick T. Terenzini. *How College Affects Students: A Third Decade of Research*. Vol.2. San Francisco: Jossey-Bass, 2005.

Pearson, Henry G. *Freshman Composition*. Boston: D.C. Heath & Co., Publishers, 1897.

Reynolds, Nedra, and Richard Aaron Rice. *Portfolio Teaching: A Guide for Instructors*. 2nd edition. Boston: Bedford/St. Martin's, 2006.

Rimer, Sara. "A Campus Fad That's Being Copied: Internet Plagiarism Seems on the Rise" September 3, 2003. *The New York Times Ethemes*. 1-3.
<http://ethemes.pearsoncmg.com/013113969X/article_09/index.html.>

Roueche, John, and Suanne Roueche. *High Stakes, High Performance: Making Remedial Education Work*. Washington, D.C.: Community College Press of the American Association of Community Colleges, 1999.

Ryan, Leigh and Lisa Zimmerelli. *The Bedford Guide for Writing Tutors*. 4th edition. Boston: Bedford/St. Martin's, 2006.

Schroeder, Jennifer L., and Harvetta Robertson. "Civility in the College Classroom." *Observer* 21.10 (November 2008): 29-31.

Shaughnessy, Mina. "Some New Approaches toward Teaching." *Teaching Developmental Writing*. 3rd edition. Ed. Susan Naomi Bernsein. Boston: Bedford/St. Martins, 2007.

Seldin, Peter. *The Teaching Portfolio: A Practical Guide to Improved Performance and Promotion/Tenure Decisions*. 3rd edition. San Francisco: Jossey-Bass, 2008.

"Study Examines the Psychology Behind Students Who Don't Cheat." *ScienceDaily* 18 August 2008. 17 October 2008 <http://www.sciencedaily.com /releases/2008/08/080817223646.htm>. 1-3.

United States. U.S. Department of Labor. Bureau of Labor Statistics. "Teachers: Post Secondary." *Occupational Outlook Handbook for 2008-2009*.
<http://www.bls.gov/oco/ocos066.htm.>

VARK: *A Guide to Learning Styles*. 2007. <http://www.vark-learn.com.>

Weimer, Maryellen. *Learner-Centered Teaching: Five Key Changes to Practice*. San Francisco: Jossey-Bass, 2002.